Wrapped in Love

GORGEOUS HAND KNITS FOR BABIES **BY FELICITY DAWSON**

PENGUIN BOOKS

Contents

Contents

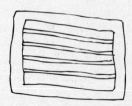

Contents

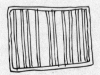   

Introduction

What could be more enjoyable than knitting cute clothes for a baby?

This book is the perfect guide to making beautiful knits for babies aged 0–12 months. Whether you're knitting for your own new baby or for a friend or family member who's expecting, there is no more heartfelt gift than something you've made yourself. With sixteen gorgeous garments and accessories to choose from, you'll find something here for every baby in your life.

Felicity Dawson has created pieces that are unique and imaginative, using colours that are rich and vibrant. In addition, she has carefully considered the needs of new parents and babies, choosing soft, natural fibres, and ensuring that each item is designed to be easy to get on and off.

There are simple patterns that are worked only in garter stitch (like the felted booties), as well as more complex designs (like the pinafore with picot frilled edge). Someone with basic knitting skills could make most of the items, but there are also more involved patterns to challenge the experienced knitter.

It's important to take good care of these special items once you've created them. Always check whether your yarns are machine washable. Most woollen fabrics should be washed by hand in cool water using wool wash, then gently squeezed out and dried flat to maintain the original shape of the garment. Never put woollen garments in the dryer as the heat will make them shrink. If storing for a long period of time, seal in a plastic bag to prevent moth damage. If looked after properly, these garments will last a lifetime.

With clear step-by-step instructions, simple charts and charming images to inspire you, *Wrapped in Love* makes it so easy to create one of these cuddly knits.

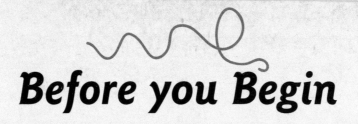

Before you Begin

Sizes

In each of the garment patterns, instructions are given for three sizes: 0–3 months, 6–9 months and 9–12 months. This table shows the measurements that these sizes are based on.

	0–3 months	6–9 months	9–12 months
Chest	42 cm (16 ½ ")	43 cm (17 ")	47.5 cm (18 ¾ ")
Waist	47 cm (18 ½ ")	48 cm (19 ")	49.5 cm (19 ½ ")
Shoulder width	20 cm (8 ")	21 cm (8 ¼ ")	23 cm (9 ")
Back of neck to waist	15.5 cm (6 ")	17.5 cm (7 ")	19 cm (7 ½ ")
Underarm length to wrist	17 cm (6 ¾ ")	19 cm (7 ½ ")	20 cm (8 ")
Upper arm circumference	13 cm (5 ")	14 cm (5 ½ ")	14.5 cm (5 ¾ ")

'Knitted measurements' indicate the finished size of the garment: the first size given is for 0–3 months, followed by 6–9 months and 9–12 months in parentheses: e.g. Chest: 48 (50, 52) cm/19 (19¾, 20½)". The same rule applies in the pattern instructions – the number of stitches or repeats varies depending on which size you are making: e.g. k8 (10, 12), p4 (6, 8).

Terms and techniques

You'll find a handy list of abbreviations at the back of the book (page 125), and all terms and techniques are listed alphabetically and explained in detail in the Terms and Techniques section on pages 114–124.

Pattern difficulty

Each pattern is rated as beginner, some experience, competent or advanced (see key below), so you can see at a glance which projects will suit you best.

Pattern difficulty			
beginner	some experience	competent	advanced

Gauge

Before beginning a pattern, it's important to knit a test swatch with your chosen yarn, wash it and block it. Measure the swatch, then adjust your needle size if necessary, to achieve the specified gauge (i.e. number of stitches and rows per 10 cm). Detailed instructions for knitting test swatches can be found under Gauge in Terms and Techniques (page 117).

All patterns in this book were created using needles with metric sizes. The needle size is given in the pattern, along with the closest US equivalent, but note that the US sizes do not correspond exactly. It's therefore doubly important for knitters using US needle sizes to check their gauge before starting a pattern.

Blocking

It is often important to block a finished piece of knitting, to give it the required shape. Directions for blocking are given in Terms and Techniques (page 114).

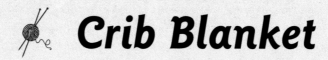

Crib Blanket

*Knitted in a simple k1, p1 rib, this blanket is so easy to make. The rib gives it a
wonderful texture and warmth, and it's easy to alter the width of the stripes if desired.
Soft and comforting, this blanket will be cherished as a precious keepsake.*

Yarn

- Eki Riva Supreme 4 ply (100% SuperBaby Alpaca;
  50 g/1¾ oz; 200 m/218 yd): 4 × balls in #2017
  magenta (MC); 3 × balls in #4659 Tyrian purple
  (A); 2 × balls in #1076 mauve (B).

Needles and notions

- 1 × 2.75 mm (US size 2) circular needle,
  80 cm (32") in length OR the size needed
  to obtain gauge

- 1 × 2.5 mm (US size C/2) crochet hook

Knitted measurements

- Approx 89 cm × 100 cm (35" × 39½")

Gauge

- 36 sts and 34 rows = 10 cm (4") in single k1, p1 rib
  without stretching.

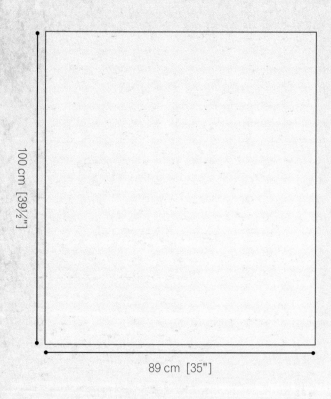

100 cm [39½"]

89 cm [35"]

BLANKET

With A, cast on 288 sts.

FOUNDATION ROW With A, *k1, p1; rep from * to end of row.

Break off A.

ROW 1 With MC, *k1, p1; rep from * to end of row.

ROW 2 As row 1.

ROW 3 With B, *k1, p1; rep from * to end of row.

ROW 4 As row 3.

Break off B.

ROW 5 With MC, *k1, p1; rep from * to end of row.

ROW 6 As row 5.

ROW 7 With A, *k1, p1; rep from * to end of row.

ROW 8 As row 7.

Break off A.

Note: The MC yarn can be carried up the side of the blanket as you will be working with it every 2 rows. The other 2 colours should be cut and the tails woven in later.

Rep these last 8 rows until blanket measures approx 100 cm (39½"). End with 1 row of A, then, still using A, cast off in rib.

FINISHING

Weave in all tails. Keep them in their colour stripes, slipping them through knit sts only, and on one side only. Cut the tails to different lengths so the woven ends won't end up all in one spot.

Edging

With A and RS facing, use the crochet hook to join yarn at right hand corner of cast-off edge.

RND 1 Ch2, 1dc into next st and then every knit st, skipping the purl sts (this prevents stretching). At corner work 3dc into the corner st, work dc down long side (approx 4 dc to every 6 knitted rows), 3dc into next corner st, 1dc into every knit st of the cast-on row (skipping the purl sts), 3dc into the corner st and dc all along the last long side in the same manner as the other long side. Join to the 2 ch sts with a
sl st.

RND 2 Ch2 (count as 1st dc in starting corner), 1dc into next st and every dc of rnd 1, working 3dc in each centre corner dc. Work 2dc in last corner dc and join to the 2 ch sts with a sl st. Fasten off.

Weave in ends and lightly block corners and edges.

Felted Booties

This is a design that is very popular in Norway. This particular version is adapted for tiny feet and is based on a pattern by Liecel Tverli Scully called 'Norwegian House Slippers', which first appeared in Volume 5 of Craft magazine.

Yarn

- Rowan Scottish Tweed 4 ply (100% pure new wool; 25 g/1 oz; 110m/120 yd): 1 × ball for booties; 1 × ball in contrast colour for pompoms. Colours used here include: #003 Skye, #005 Lavender, #011 Sunset, #015 Apple, #016 Thistle, #020 Mallard, #021 Winter Navy, #026 Rose.

Needles and notions

- 1 × pair 4 mm (US size 6) needles

- 12 × small safety pins or small removable markers or lengths of contrast thread

Finished size

- To fit foot approx 9–12 cm (3½–4½") in length

Gauge

- *See Special Instructions: Test Swatch (page 10).*

Note

- The booties are knitted in one piece marked into 8 'squares', which when folded and stitched forms the bootie shape. It is very important that you place the markers as indicated in the pattern, so that you have the 'squares' clearly marked out for folding. It may be helpful to thread small lengths of different coloured yarns along the sides of each square: e.g. red at A and a, yellow at B and b, and so on.

Special Instructions

TEST SWATCH

Before you begin, it's a good idea to make a test square to ensure you end up with the desired finished size. Cast on 10 sts and knit 20 rows. Felt it as in the instructions (page 11). When dry, measure the diagonal – the sole of the finished bootie will be slightly less than double that measurement (so it should be 5–7 cm (2–2¾"), depending on your preferred finished size). Adjustments to size can be made with further testing, either by using larger knitting needles or knitting a larger piece with extra rows and sts – e.g. cast on 11 sts and knit 22 rows. Note that for every extra st added, you will need to add 2 extra rows to each 'square'.

BOOTIES *(make 2 the same)*

Cast on 10 sts and knit 100 rows, placing a marker at each end of every 20th row.

Knit another 20 rows, then cast off 9 sts but do not break yarn.

Turn the work so that the long side lies to your left and the last loop still on your needle is on your right *(see Figure 1)*.

Now pick up and knit 9 more sts along the long side (picking up between knit ridges), which will bring you to the last left hand side marker you placed at row 100 *(see Figure 2)*. On these 10 sts, knit 40 rows, placing a marker at each end of the 20th row worked. Cast off.

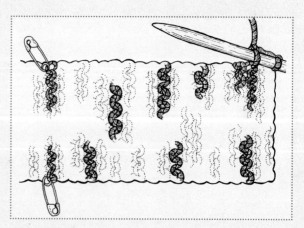

Figure 1

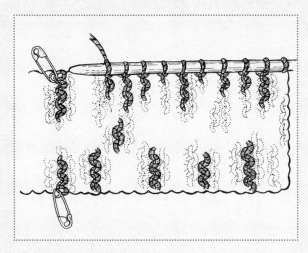

Figure 2

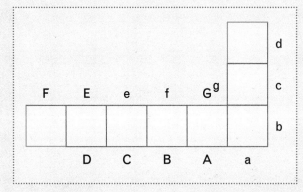

Figure 3

MAKING UP

Place this L-shape in front of you with the long side to your left and the short side going straight up *(see Figure 3)*.

Now fold the short side (with 3 squares) over to the left so that **a** is on top of **A**. Using an overcast sewing stitch, sew **a** to **A**. Manipulate the corner, twisting the work slightly, to continue sewing **b** to **B**, **c** to **C** and **d** to **D**. Fasten off. Now fold **e** to **E** and **f** to **F** and sew them tog. Fasten off. The last sides to be sewn tog are **g** to **G**. (The sides marked blue on the diagram are not sewn – they form the 'collar' of the bootie, where the foot goes in.) Weave in any tails.

FELTING

Felting can be done in a washing machine or by hand. I've found it's easier to control the sizing of these tiny booties when I felt by hand, and although it takes a bit more elbow grease, it actually takes less time (and uses far less water!).

Felting by hand (preferred method)

STEP 1 Put a small amount of extremely hot water into a metal pot, along with a squirt of dishwashing

liquid. Add the booties, along with a rough tea towel (linen is good).

STEP 2 Wearing rubber gloves, agitate the pot contents with a wooden spoon and occasionally squeeze and rub the booties with your hands. Do this for 5 minutes.

STEP 3 Throw the booties into a bucket of cold water to shock the fibres into shrinking, then squeeze out excess moisture.

STEP 4 Add more really hot water to the pot and agitate the booties for another 5 minutes.

STEP 5 Repeat step 3. The booties should now be very close to the desired finished size, but if necessary you can repeat step 4 and then step 3 once more.

STEP 6 When the booties look like they're close to the size you want, submerge them in cold water to which you've added a dash of vinegar (this stops the felting process). Rinse well, removing all traces of soap (if they are not thoroughly rinsed, the residual soap may cause the fabric to rot).

STEP 7 Blot the booties dry with a towel and push and pull them into their finished shape.

Felting in a washing machine

(This method is recommended only if you are felting multiple pairs of booties at once.)

Front-loading washing machines generally don't work for felting, as you aren't able to keep checking the garment throughout the process. This is especially true if you want to end up with a garment of a particular size. Therefore, these instructions are for top-loaders.

STEP 1 Fill your washing machine to the lowest level with the hottest water and add a small amount of dishwashing liquid (which encourages the felting process by softening the fibres).

STEP 2 Add the booties to the wash, plus a pair of old jeans (make sure they're colourfast) to help speed the felting process. (You may wish to put the booties in a pillowcase to protect them.)

STEP 3 Keep washing until the booties are felted to the size you want, without letting the machine move into spin or rinse mode. (You may need to run the longest wash cycle 2 or 3 times.) Check on the progress of the felting often. After the first 10 minutes or so the booties may actually appear to stretch, but then the felting process will begin.

(Be careful not to let the booties shrink too much
– you can always run the felting process again to
shrink them more, but not the other way round!)

Step 4 When the booties look about the right size
(you get a better idea if you squeeze the excess
water from them), remove from the washing
machine and submerge in a bucket of cold water
to which you've added a dash of white vinegar (this
stops the felting process). Rinse well, removing all
traces of soap (if they are not thoroughly rinsed, the
residual soap may cause the fabric to rot).

Step 5 Blot the booties dry with a towel and pull
and push them into their finished shape.

POMPOMS *(make 2)*

The easiest way to make pompoms is with a
commercial pompom maker (available from crafting
and fabric stores). Simply follow the instructions
included.

If you don't have a pompom maker, you can make
your own. Cut out 2 rounds of cardboard, each with
a diameter of 8 cm, then cut a round hole with a
diameter of 3 cm in the centre of each piece. Hold
the 2 pieces of cardboard together and wrap yarn
around both pieces, passing it through the hole

in the centre, until you have a thick layer of yarn
completely covering the cardboard (the more yarn
you wind the thicker your pompom will be). Holding
the pieces of card together firmly, carefully cut the
yarn all the way around the outside edge. Thread a
long piece of strong cotton or string between the
2 pieces of card and wrap around several times,
pulling it tight and securing firmly with a double
knot. Remove the pieces of card and shape the
pompom into a ball, trimming any stray threads
to create an even surface.

FINISHING

Sew a pompom to the top of each bootie.

 # *Cable Vest*

This cabled vest is so versatile. Pair it with a short-sleeved or long-sleeved top, depending on the weather; choose a simple t-shirt or grow-suit for everyday wear, or dress it up with a pretty floral shirt.

Yarn

- Filatura di Crosa Zarina (100% merino extra-fine; 50 g/1¾ oz; 165 m/180 yd): 2 × balls in #1759 khaki (MC); 1 × ball in #1740 coral (CC).

Needles and notions

- 1 × pair 3 mm (US size 3) needles OR the size needed to obtain gauge
- 1 × 2.5 mm (US size C/2) crochet hook
- 1 × cable needle
- 1 × stitch holder
- row counters
- 1 × wool needle
- 2 × 12 mm (½") buttons

Sizes

- 0–3 months (6–9 months, 9–12 months)

Knitted measurements

- Chest: 52 (53, 54) cm/20.5 (21, 21.5)"
- Length from top of shoulder: 27 (28.5, 31) cm/ 10.5 (11.5, 12.5)"

Gauge

- 26 sts and 36 rows = 10 cm (4") in pattern after blocking.
- 23 sts and 34 rows = 10 cm (4") in st st.

Notes

- It is very important to keep track of both the pattern repeat row numbers and the rows worked in each pattern piece. A multi-stitch counter is very helpful for this pattern.
- The cable rib pattern is very stretchy and needs to be blocked to obtain the finished measurements.

FRONT

Using CC, cast on 66 (68, 70) sts.

SET UP ROW (WS) P4 (5, 6), *k3, p8; rep from *
to end of row, ending last rep k3, p4 (5, 6).
Break off CC. Join in MC and work with it to
completion of piece.

Begin cable pattern *(see chart)*

ROW 1 (RS) K4 (5, 6), *p3, k8; rep from * to end
of row, ending last rep p3, k4 (5, 6).

ROW 2 K2 (3, 4), p2, *k3, p2, k4, p2; rep from *
to end of row, ending last rep k3, p2, k2 (3, 4).

ROW 3 As row 1.

ROW 4 As row 2.

ROW 5 As row 1.

ROW 6 As row 2.

ROW 7 As row 1.

ROW 8 P4 (5, 6), *k3, p8; rep from * to end of row,
ending last rep k3, p4 (5, 6).

ROW 9 K4 (5, 6), *p3, k8; rep from * to end of row,
ending last rep p3, k4 (5, 6).

ROW 10 As row 8.

ROW 11 K0 (1, 2), c4L, *p3, c4R, c4L; rep from *
to end of row, ending last rep p3, c4R, k0 (1, 2).

ROW 12 P4 (5, 6), *k3, p8; rep from * to end of row,

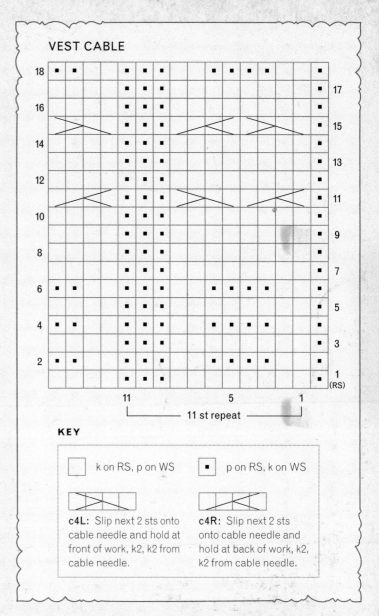

VEST CABLE

11 st repeat

KEY

| | k on RS, p on WS | ▪ | p on RS, k on WS |

c4L: Slip next 2 sts onto cable needle and hold at front of work, k2, k2 from cable needle.

c4R: Slip next 2 sts onto cable needle and hold at back of work, k2, k2 from cable needle.

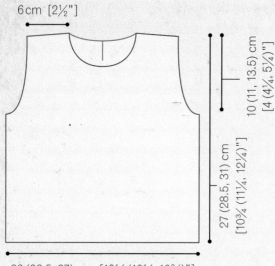

6 cm [2½"]

10 (11, 13.5) cm [4 (4¼, 5¼)"]

27 (28.5, 31) cm [10¾ (11¼, 12¼)"]

26 (26.5, 27) cm [10¼ (10½, 10¾)"]

These 18 rows set the pattern. Rep them until 58 (62, 66) rows have been worked – work measures approx 16 (17.5, 18.5) cm/6¼ (7, 7¼)" from cast-on edge.

Armhole shaping
Cast off 4 (3, 3) sts at beg of next 2 rows.
0–3 months Dec 1 st at each end of rows 62 and 66 – 54 sts rem.
6–9 months Dec 1 st at each end of rows 66, 70 and 76 – 56 sts rem.
9–12 months Dec 1 st at each end of rows 72, 76 and 78 – 58 sts rem.
Continue to work in pattern as set until 80 (88, 94) rows have been worked from cast-on edge.

Begin neck shaping
Row 1 Patt 22 (23, 24), cast off 10, patt 22 (23, 24). Turn and work on these last 22 (23, 24) sts worked. (Make a note of both the pattern repeat and the row number at this point, so the left shoulder can be started on the matching row.)

Right neck edge
Row 2 Patt to end of row.

ending last rep k3, p4 (5, 6).
Row 13 K4 (5, 6), *p3, k8; rep from * to end of row, ending last rep p3, k4 (5, 6).
Row 14 As row 12.
Row 15 K0 (1, 2), c4R, *p3, c4L, c4R; rep from * to end of row, ending last rep p3, c4L, k0 (1, 2).
Row 16 As row 12.
Row 17 K4 (5, 6), *p3, k8; rep from * to end of row, ending last rep p3, k4 (5, 6).
Row 18 K2 (3, 4), p2, *k3, p2, k4, p2; rep from * to end of row, ending last rep k3, p2, k2 (3, 4).

Row 3 Dec 1 st at beg of row (neck edge).

0–3 months Cont in patt, dec 1 st at neck edge on rows 84, 85, 86, 88, 91 – 16 sts rem.

6–9 months Cont in patt, dec 1 st at neck edge on rows 92, 93, 95, 97, 101 – 17 sts rem.

9–12 months Cont in patt, dec 1 st at neck edge on rows 98, 99, 101, 103, 105 – 18 sts rem.

Work without shaping in patt until 94 (102, 110) rows from cast-on edge have been completed. Cast off loosely.

Left neck edge

Rejoin yarn at neck edge with WS facing you, and work as for right neck edge from Row 2, matching patt to right neck and reversing any shaping.

BACK

Work as for front until 77 (87, 93) rows have been completed, finishing on a RS row.

Left back with buttonband

NEXT ROW (WS) Work 27 (28, 29) sts for left shoulder. Work the remaining sts, then place these 27 (28, 29) sts on a stitch holder for the right shoulder.

Turn work and cable cast on 5 sts at beg of row for buttonband – 32 (33, 34) sts on needle. Knit these 5 sts and patt to end of row.

NEXT ROW Patt to last 5 sts, k5.

Cont to work in patt without shaping, knitting the 5 buttonband sts on every row, until 90 (100, 106) rows have been completed. Work appropriate cables as you come to them.

NEXT ROW At neck edge, cast off 10 (14, 16) sts, patt to end of row – 22 (19, 18) sts rem.

NEXT ROW Patt to end of row.

NEXT ROW (NECK EDGE) Cast off 6 (2, 2) sts, patt to end of row – 16 (17, 16) sts rem.
NEXT ROW Patt to end of row.
Cast off all the 16 (17, 16) sts loosely.

Right back with buttonholes
With WS facing, rejoin yarn at the centre back, and patt the sts from the stitch holder. Beg at row 78 (88, 94) of the back piece, cast on 1 st at beg of row and patt to end of row 28 (29, 30) sts. (Knit this st every row until neck cast off.)
NEXT ROW (RS) Patt to last st, k1.
NEXT ROW K1, patt to end of row.
NEXT ROW (RS) (1ST BUTTONHOLE) Patt until 3 sts rem, yo, k2tog, k1.
NEXT ROW K1, patt to end of row (working yo from previous row as a st).
Cont in patt, knitting edge st as set until 87 (97, 103) rows have been worked from cast-on edge.
NEXT ROW (WS) (2ND BUTTONHOLE) K1, k2tog, yo, patt to end of row.
NEXT ROW Patt to last st, k1 (working yo from previous row as a st). (Note that for **9–12 months** this row – row 105 – is a c4L row. Work cable as usual.)

Work without shaping, until 91 (101, 107) rows are complete.
NEXT ROW (NECK EDGE) Cast off 6 (10, 12) sts, patt to end of row – 22 (19, 18) sts rem.
NEXT ROW Patt to end of row.
NEXT ROW Cast off 6 (2, 2) sts, patt to end of row. Cast off all 16 (17, 16) sts loosely.

FINISHING AND NECKBAND
Weave in all ends. Block pieces to finished measurements (don't press the cables flat).
Using mattress st, sew shoulder seams. Pin the bottom of the buttonband into place on the WS of the right back and sew in position. Sew side seams.

With crochet hook and CC, work 1 row of dc around neck only. Fasten off and weave in ends. Sew buttons on buttonband to match buttonholes.

Cable Vest

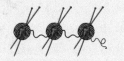 # Wrap with Side Ties

The body of this wrap is made in a single piece, knitted back and forth on a circular needle. The side ties make it adjustable, so it will fit Baby for many months.

Yarn

- Filatura di Crosa Zarina (100% merino extra-fine; 50 g/1¾ oz; 165 m/180 yd): 3 × balls in #1469 dark-grey (MC); 1 × ball in #1449 bright-red (CC).

Needles and notions

- 2 × 3 mm (US size 3) circular needles, 80 cm (32") in length OR the size needed to obtain gauge
- 2 × 2.5 mm (US size 1 or 2) dpn
- markers
- 1 × row counter
- 1 × wool needle

Sizes

- 0–3 months (6–9 months, 9–12 months)

Knitted measurements

- Chest: 48 (50, 52) cm/19 (19¾, 20½)"
- Length from top of shoulder: 27.5 (28.5, 31) cm/10¾ (11¼, 12¼)"
- Length of sleeve from underarm: 18 (20, 22) cm/7 (8, 8¾)"

Gauge

- 23 sts and 34 rows = 10 cm (4") in st st.

Note

- An alternative to the provisional cast-on is to crochet a chain in a contrast yarn – the same number of links for each st required plus 1. Cut yarn and pull last loop. With MC, pick up a st from each link (this must be done from the loop at the back of the link). Don't pick up the last link. This row is counted as 1 knit row. The advantage of this method is that it unravels easily when required – just undo and pull back the last link.

BODY

Hem

Start with a provisional cast-on. With contrasting scrap yarn and using thumb method cast on 176 (182, 186) sts. Cut yarn leaving a tail. Join in MC.

Row 1 Purl.

Row 2 Knit.

Row 3 Purl.

Row 4 Knit.

Row 5 (HEM FOLDOVER ROW) Knit.

Row 6 Knit.

Row 7 Purl.

Row 8 Knit.

Row 9 Purl.

Now carefully unravel the provisional cast-on sts and place the free loops on the spare 80 cm (32") circular needle. Fold hem over and, holding the needle with the unravelled loops at the back of your work, knit tog 1 st from each needle, until all sts have been knitted tog. (This can be slippery work and sts fall off the needle tips easily, so work slowly to avoid any problems.)

Purl 1 row – hem is complete.

Begin main body

Row 1 (RS) Knit.

Row 2 Purl.

Row 3 Knit.

Row 4 Purl.

Row 5 Knit.

Row 6 Purl.

Row 7 Knit.

Row 8 Purl.

Row 9 (1ST DEC ROW) K54 (56, 57), ssk, pm, k1, k2tog, k58 (60, 62), ssk, pm, k1, k2tog, k54 (56, 57) – 4 sts decreased and 172 (178, 182) sts rem.

Cont in st st until 24 rows have been worked.

Row 25 (2ND DEC ROW) Knit to 2 sts before 1st marker, ssk, sm, k1, k2tog, knit to last 2 sts before 2nd marker, ssk, sm, k1, k2tog, knit to end – 4 sts decreased and 168 (174, 178) sts rem.

Cont without shaping in st st until 40 rows have been worked.

Row 41 (3RD DEC ROW) Dec as row 25 – 4 sts decreased and 164 (170, 174) sts rem.

Cont in st st until 42 (44, 46) rows have been worked.

Begin neck shaping

Row 1 (RS) Cast off 10 sts, knit to 5 sts before 1st marker, yf, k2tog (this is the buttonhole for tie), knit to end of row – 154 (160, 164) sts rem.

Row 2 Cast off 10 sts, purl to end of row (working yo from previous row as a new st).

Row 3 Cast off 3 sts, knit to end of row.

Row 4 Cast off 3 sts, purl to end of row.

Row 5 Cast off 4 (3, 3) sts, knit to end of row.

Row 6 Cast off 4 (3, 3) sts, purl to end of row.

Row 7 Ssk, knit to last 2 sts, k2tog.

Row 8 Purl.

Row 9 Ssk, knit to last 2 sts, k2tog.

Row 10 P2tog, purl to last 2 sts, ssp.

Rep these last 2 rows 3 (5, 5) times more, then row 9 once more – 110 (110, 114) sts.

NEXT ROW (WS) Purl.

Begin raglan armhole shaping

NEXT ROW Ssk, knit to 1 st before 1st marker, cast off 2 sts, one either side of marker, removing marker as you go, knit to 2nd marker, remove and cast off next 2 sts *after* marker, knit to last 2 sts, k2tog – 104 (108, 108) sts rem. Place each of the 1st 2 sets of sts onto stitch holders (for the back and right front).

Left front

Work on last set of sts for left front – 24 (23, 24) sts on needle.

Row 1 (WS) Purl to last st, k1.

Row 2 P1, ssk, knit to last 2 sts, k2tog.

Rep these 2 rows 5 times more.

Cont to dec at armhole edge only on every RS row, AND AT THE SAME TIME dec at neck edge every 4th (4th, 6th) row 2 (4, 3) times more.

Cont to dec at armhole edge only on every RS row until 2 sts rem. K2tog and pull loop up and fasten off.

Right front

Rejoin yarn at underarm edge of right front with WS facing you.

Row 1 K1, purl to end of row.

Row 2 Ssk, knit to last 3 sts, k2tog, p1.

Using the dec slanting as set in row 2, complete right front as for left front, reversing shaping.

Back

With WS facing you, rejoin yarn at left back and purl 1 row.

NEXT ROW (RS) P1, ssk, knit to last 3 sts, k2tog, p1.

NEXT ROW K1, purl to last st, k1.

Wrap with Side Ties

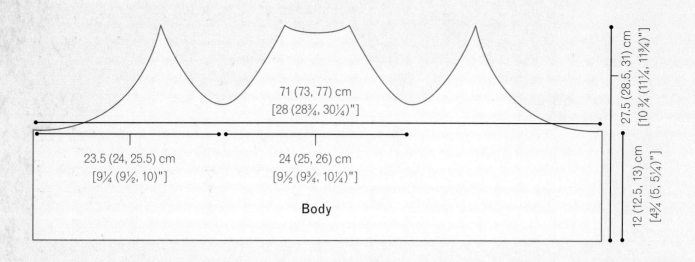

71 (73, 77) cm
[28 (28¾, 30¼)"]

27.5 (28.5, 31) cm
[10 ¾ (11¼, 11¾)"]

23.5 (24, 25.5) cm
[9¼ (9½, 10)"]

24 (25, 26) cm
[9½ (9¾, 10¼)"]

Body

12 (12.5, 13) cm
[4¾ (5, 5¼)"]

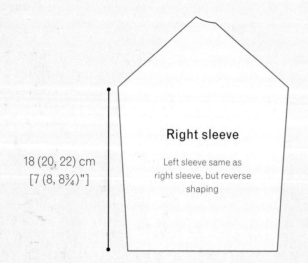

Right sleeve

Left sleeve same as
right sleeve, but reverse
shaping

18 (20, 22) cm
[7 (8, 8¾)"]

Rep these last 2 rows until 26 sts rem. Cast off.

RIGHT SLEEVE

With scrap contrasting yarn, make a provisional cast-on of 38 (40, 42) sts. Cut yarn.
Join in MC.

Hem

Row 1 Purl.

Row 2 Knit.

Row 3 Purl.

Row 4 Knit.

Row 5 (HEM FOLDOVER ROW) Knit.

Hem will be completed after sleeve seam is sewn.

Main sleeve shaping

Row 1 (RS) Knit.

Row 2 Purl.

Row 3 Knit.

Row 4 Purl.

Row 5 Knit.

Row 6 Purl.

Row 7 Knit.

Row 8 Purl.

Row 9 (1ST INC ROW) Inc in 1st and last st.

Cont to work in st st, inc in 1st and last st of every foll 12th (14th, 14th) row 4 times more — 48 (50, 52) sts.
Cont without shaping until work measures 18.5 (20, 22) cm/7¼ (8, 8¾)" from hem foldover row.

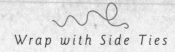

Raglan armhole shaping

Row 1 (RS) P1, ssk, knit to last 3 sts, k2tog, p1.

Row 2 K1, p2tog, purl to last 3 sts, ssp, k1.

Rep these 2 rows until 10 sts rem, ending on a RS row.

Sleeve cap

Next row K1, p2tog, purl to end of row.

Next row Cast off 6 sts, sl the last st worked on right hand needle back onto the left hand needle, k2tog, p1.

Next row P2tog, draw up loop and fasten off.

LEFT SLEEVE

Work as for right sleeve until 10 sts rem.

Sleeve cap

Next row (WS) Cast off 6 sts, ssp over the next 2 sts, k1.

Next row P1, ssk.

Next row P2tog, draw up loop and fasten off.

FINISHING

Block all pieces. Sew sleeve seams using mattress stitch, but don't catch the contrast yarn ends of the provisional cast-on in the seam. Carefully unravel provisional cast-on sts and place on 2 circular needles. Fold over hem to WS, thread a wool needle with MC and with an overcast sewing stitch, sew each unravelled loop onto the main sleeve. (This may be awkward but just move a few sts forward at a time, pushing the sts to the needle tip as you go.) Pin underarm seam of each sleeve into place and then pin the sleeve to fit the body (the high side of the raglan sleeve goes towards the back). Using mattress st, sew the seam through the edge st of the raglan shaping.

Neckband

With CC and RS facing you, beg at right front edge of neck shaping, pick up and knit 51 (51, 56) sts up front right neck, 6 across top of right sleeve, 24 across back neck, 6 across top of left sleeve, 51 (51, 56) down left front neck – 138 (138, 148) sts.

Working back and forth on the circular needle, starting with a purl row, work in st st for 5 rows.

NEXT ROW Sl next st onto right hand needle, pick up corresponding loop at back from 1st CC pick-up row 5 rows below, put left tip into front of slipped st (2nd from right hand tip) and through picked-up st. Knit both loops tog as 1 st. Rep once more then pass 1st st over 2nd st. Cont to end of row and fasten off.

Weave CC threads in. To keep the neck piping lying flat, use MC to sew it down with an overcast sewing stitch, picking up the two CC chain loops of each st and sewing them to the MC knitted garment. Make sure the sewing yarn doesn't go through to the RS of wrap.

Ties (make 4)

With CC and dpn, cast on 3 sts, leaving a tail long enough to sew the tie onto the garment later. Knit 1st row, then, without turning work, push sts to the right hand end of the needle, and knit with the other needle, pulling the yarn from behind. Cont knitting in this way until the cord is 18 cm (7") long. Cut yarn, leaving a tail. Thread the tail through a wool needle and draw the threaded needle through the 3 sts on the knitting needle, pulling tightly as you drop them off the needle. Now make 1 or 2 sts to

fasten firmly, thread the yarn down into the cord as far as you can and cut yarn.

Sew 1 tie at each end of neckband. Sew the other 2 ties at the 'side' seams about 5 cm (2") below underarm, to match up with neckband ties.

All-in-one Striped Jumper

This jumper is simple and quick to knit as it is worked in one piece using only garter stitch. There is a buttoned opening across one shoulder, to make it easy to get on and off.

Yarn

- Grignasco Bambi (100% merino extra-fine; 50 g/1¾ oz; 225 m/246 yd): 1 × ball in #680 watermelon (MC); 1 × ball in #787 light-grey (A); 1 × ball in #671 hot-pink (B).

Needles and notions

- 1 × 3 mm (US size 3) circular needle, 60 cm in length OR the size needed to obtain gauge
- 3 × stitch holders
- markers
- 1 × row counter
- 1 × wool needle
- 2 × 12–15 mm (5/8") buttons

Sizes

- 0–3 months (6–9 months, 9–12 months)

Knitted measurements

- Chest: 48 (51, 56) cm/19 (20, 22)"
- Length from top of shoulder: 26 (28, 30) cm/10¼ (11, 12)"
- Sleeve length from underarm: 17 (19.5, 23) cm/6¾ (7¾, 9)"

Gauge

- 26 sts and 52 rows = 10 cm (4") in garter stitch.

Notes

- Jumper is knitted in one piece, starting at the lower front edge and ending at the lower back edge. It's easiest to use a circular needle, working back and forth.

- All rows are knit stitch only (garter stitch) and new colours are introduced on the RS only. Only the WS of the jumper will show the colour change ridges.

BUTTONBAND

With MC, cast on 16 sts.

Rows 1–6 Knit.

Row 7 (RS) Knit to last 2 sts, k2tog. (This dec end is the neck edge.)

Row 8 Knit.

Row 9 Knit to last 2 sts, k2tog.

Row 10 Knit.

Break off yarn leaving a tail about 30 cm (12") long and place these 14 sts on a stitch holder for later.

BODY

Begin lower front edge

0–3 months Using MC cast on 60 sts.

6–9 months Using MC, cast on 64 sts and knit 2 rows. Then knit 2 rows in A.

9–12 months Using MC, cast on 70 sts and knit 4 rows. Then knit 2 rows in B, 2 rows in A, 2 rows in MC.

All sizes Cont to knit without shaping to the underarm in the following colour sequence:
4 rows in MC; 4 rows in A; 2 rows in B; 6 rows in MC; 2 rows in A; 2 rows in B; 4 rows in A; 6 rows in MC; 2 rows in A; 4 rows in MC; 4 rows in B; 4 rows in A; 2 rows in MC; 2 rows in A; 6 rows in MC; 4 rows in A; 2 rows in B; 4 rows in A; 6 rows in MC – 70 (74, 80) rows from cast-on edge.

Increases for sleeves

0–3 months With B, cast on 5 sts at beg of next 2 rows – 70 sts.

With A, cast on 5 sts at beg of next 4 rows – 90 sts.

With MC, cast on 5 sts at beg of next 6 rows – 120 sts.

With A, cast on 5 sts at beg of next 2 rows – 130 sts.

With MC, cast on 4 sts at beg of next 4 rows – 146 sts.

Cont as for **all sizes** (next page).

6–9 months With B, cast on 5 sts at beg of next
2 rows – 74 sts.

With A, cast on 5 sts at beg of next 4 rows – 94 sts.

With MC, cast on 5 sts at beg of next 6 rows –
124 sts.

With A, cast on 5 sts at beg of next 2 rows – 134 sts.

Still with A, cast on 4 sts at beg of next 2 rows –
142 sts.

With MC, cast on 4 sts at beg of next 4 rows –
158 sts.

Cont as for **all sizes** (next column).

9–12 months With B, cast on 5 sts at beg of next
2 rows – 80 sts.

With A, cast on 5 sts at beg of next 4 rows – 100 sts.

With MC, cast on 5 sts at beg of next 6 rows – 130
sts.

With A, cast on 5 sts at beg of next 2 rows – 140 sts.

With B, cast on 4 sts at beg of next 2 rows – 148 sts.

With A, cast on 4 sts at beg of next 2 rows – 156 sts.

With MC, cast on 4 sts at beg of next 4 rows –
172 sts.

Cont as for **all sizes** (next column).

All sizes Work straight without shaping on these
146 (158, 172) sts in the foll colour sequence:
2 rows in B; 4 rows in MC; 2 rows in A; 2 rows in B;
4 rows in A; 6 rows in MC; 4 rows in A; 2 rows in
MC – 114 (120, 128) rows from cast-on edge.

Right neck and shoulder shaping

Row 1 With MC, k71 (76, 83), cast off 4 (6, 6) sts,
knit to end of row. There are now 71 (76, 83) sts on
either side of cast-off sts. Work on these last 71
(76, 83) sts (right shoulder) and place other sts on
holder (for left shoulder).

Row 2 (ws) Still with MC, knit to neck edge.

Row 3 Cast off 7 sts (**all sizes**) and knit to end
of row.

Row 4 Knit.

Row 5 With B, k2tog, knit to end of row.

Row 6 With B, knit.

Row 7 With A, k2tog, knit to end of row.

Row 8 With A, knit.

Row 9 With MC, k2tog, knit to end of row.

Row 10 With MC, knit.

Rows 11 & 12 With MC, knit.

Rows 13 & 14 With A, knit.

Row 15 With A, inc 1 st at neck edge, knit to end.

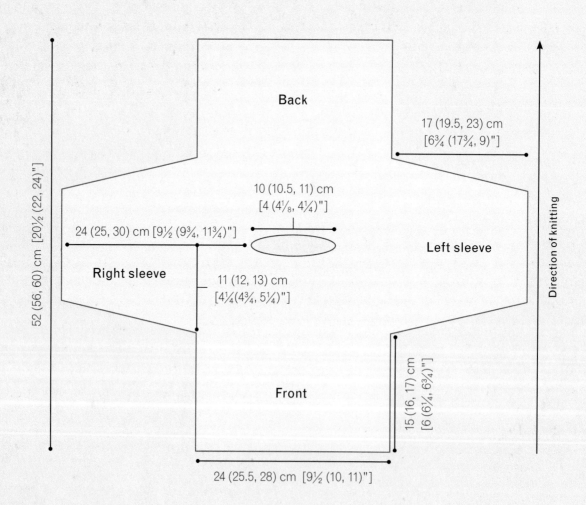

Back

17 (19.5, 23) cm
[6¾ (17¾, 9)"]

10 (10.5, 11) cm
[4 (4⅛, 4¼)"]

24 (25, 30) cm [9½ (9¾, 11¾)"]

Left sleeve

Right sleeve

11 (12, 13) cm
[4¼ (4¾, 5¼)"]

52 (56, 60) cm [20½ (22, 24)"]

Direction of knitting

Front

15 (16, 17) cm
[6 (6¼, 6¾)"]

24 (25.5, 28) cm [9½ (10, 11)"]

Row 16 With A, knit.

Row 17 With MC, inc in 1st st, knit to end of row.

Row 18 With MC, knit.

Rows 19 & 20 As rows 17 and 18.

Once row 20 has been completed, turn work and cable cast-on 7 sts for back neck. Slip these sts for right side onto a stitch holder for later. Cut yarn, leaving a long tail.

Left neck and shoulder shaping

(See Special Instructions: Make Buttonhole)

Slip left hand shoulder sts from stitch holder onto circular needle – 71 (76, 83) sts on needle.

Starting from Row 2 as in right shoulder, work as follows:

Row 2 Rejoin MC at neck edge (WS facing you), cable cast-on 7 sts and knit to end of row.

Row 3 Still with MC, knit.

Row 4 K3 tog, knit to end of row.

Row 5 With B, knit.

Row 6 With B, k2tog, k4, make buttonhole, k4, make buttonhole, knit to end of row.

Row 7 With A, knit.

Row 8 With A, k2tog, knit to end of row.

Rows 9–11 With MC, knit.

Special Instructions

MAKE BUTTONHOLE

(This is a single row reinforced buttonhole.)

STEP 1 Sl 1 pwise with yf.

STEP 2 Yb and leave it there.

STEP 3 *Sl 1 pwise, pass previous st over it; rep from * with next st.

STEP 4 Sl the last st back onto left needle and turn work.

STEP 5 Yb.

STEP 6 Cable cast-on 2 sts.

STEP 7 Cable cast-on 1 more st but yf before placing it on left hand needle, turn work.

STEP 8 Sl 1 kwise and pass extra cable st over it, then knit to end of row.

Row 12 With MC, cast off 14 sts, knit to end of row.

Row 13 With A, knit to end of row, then knit across 14 sts of buttonband (from stitch holder) with the decreased sts end at neck edge.

Rows 14–16 With A, knit.

Row 17 With MC, knit.

Row 18 With MC, inc in 1st st, knit to end of row.

Row 19 With MC, knit.

Row 20 With MC, inc in 1st st, knit to end of row.

Next row (RS) With MC, knit to end of row, ending at neck edge. Turn work and cable cast-on 11 sts. Turn work back so that the RS is facing you again, with the cast-on sts at the tip of the right hand needle. The yarn will be hanging at the back of the last st cast on. Now knit the sts for the right side from the stitch holder, making sure the RS of work is facing you and the work isn't twisted. The first sts you will knit will be the 7 cast-on sts previously made but not yet knitted. Continue to knit to end of row – 146 (158, 172) sts.

Next row (WS) With MC, knit all sts.

Back sleeve
All sizes Work without shaping in the following colour sequence:
2 rows in B; 4 rows in A; 2 rows in B; 2 rows in A; 6 rows in MC; 4 rows in A; 4 rows in MC; 2 rows in A.

Sleeve shaping decreases
0–3 months With MC, cast off 4 sts at beg of next 4 rows – 130 sts rem.

With B, cast off 5 sts at beg of next 4 rows – 110 sts rem.

With A, cast off 5 sts at beg of next 4 rows – 90 sts rem.

With MC, cast off 5 sts at beg of next 4 rows – 70 sts rem.

With A, cast off 5 sts at beg of next 2 rows – 60 sts rem.

Cont as for **all sizes** (page 38).

6–9 months With MC, cast off 4 sts at beg of next 4 rows – 142 sts rem.

With B, cast off 4 sts at beg of next 2 rows – 134 sts rem.

Still with B, cast off 5 sts at beg of next 2 rows – 124 sts rem.

With A, cast off 5 sts at beg of next 4 rows – 104 sts rem.

With MC, cast off 5 sts at beg of next 6 rows – 74 sts rem.

With A, cast off 5 sts at beg of next 2 rows – 64 sts rem.

Cont as for **all sizes** (page 38).

9–12 months With MC, cast off 4 sts at beg of next 4 rows – 156 sts rem.

With B, cast off 4 sts at beg of next 4 rows – 140 sts rem.

With A, cast off 5 sts at beg of next 4 rows – 120 sts rem.

With MC, cast off 5 sts at beg of next 2 rows – 110 sts rem.

With B, cast off 5 sts at beg of next 2 rows – 100 sts rem.

With MC, cast off 5 sts at beg of next 4 rows – 80 sts rem.

With A, cast off 5 sts at beg of next 2 rows – 70 sts rem.

Cont as for **all sizes** (page 38).

Back underarm to lower back edge

This is worked in reverse of the front stripe
sequence so the stripes will match at the side seam.

All sizes Cont to work without shaping on the 60
(64, 70) sts, in the foll order:

6 rows in MC; 4 rows in A; 2 rows in B; 4 rows in A;
6 rows in MC; 2 rows in A; 2 rows in MC; 4 rows in
A; 4 rows in B; 4 rows in MC; 2 rows in A; 6 rows in
MC; 4 rows in A; 2 rows in B; 2 rows in A; 6 rows in
MC; 2 rows in B; 4 rows in A; 4 rows in MC.

After the last 4 rows of MC:

0–3 months Cast off using elastic cast-off.

6–9 months Knit the foll extra rows: 2 rows in A;
2 rows in MC. Cast off using elastic cast-off.

9–12 months Knit the foll extra rows: 2 rows in MC;
2 rows in A; 2 rows in B; 4 rows in MC. Cast off
using elastic cast-off.

NECKBAND AND FINISHING

With RS of jumper facing you, begin at the top left
hand shoulder and using B and circular needle,
pick up and knit 31 sts evenly around front neckline
to top of right shoulder, 33 sts around back neckline
to top of left shoulder and 6 sts down the neck edge
of the buttonband – 70 sts.

Knit 1 row.

Cast off using elastic cast-off.

Matching side stripes, sew side and sleeve seams
using mattress st. Catch down buttonband on
wrong side with a few stitches. Sew on buttons
to match buttonholes.

Note: There is no need to block a garment knitted
in garter st as all the edges lie flat.

 **Hoodie**

Everyone loves a hoodie – they're so cosy and easy to wear – and now Baby can have one too!

Yarn

- Jo Sharp Silkroad DK Tweed (85% wool, 10% silk, 5% cashmere; 50 g/1¾ oz; 135 m/147 yd): 4 × balls in #410 berry.

Needles and notions

- 1 × pair 4 mm (US size 6) needles OR the size needed to obtain gauge

- 1 × cable needle

- 1 × stitch holder

- markers

- 1 × row counter

- 1 × wool needle

- 5 × 15–18 mm (½–⅞") buttons or toggle buttons

Sizes

- 0–3 months (6–9 months, 9–12 months)

Knitted measurements

- Chest: 56 (60, 61) cm/22 (23½, 24)"

- Length from top of shoulder: 30 (32.5, 35) cm/ 11¾ (12¾, 13¾)"

- Sleeve length from underarm: 18 (20, 22.5) cm/ 7 (8, 9)"

Gauge

- 18 sts and 26 rows = 10 cm (4") over cable pattern.

Notes

- Cables are very stretchy and pieces must be blocked to obtain finished measurements.

- On the row after a buttonhole row, work the yo, when you come to it, as a stitch.

BACK

Cast on 50 (52, 54) sts and knit 6 rows.

Begin cable pattern (*see chart*):

ROW I (RS) P4 (5, 6), *k2, p2, k4, p2; rep from *
3 times more, k2, p4 (5, 6).

ROW 2 K4 (5, 6), *p2, k2, k4, k2; rep from * 3 times
more, p2, k4 (5, 6).

Rep rows 1 and 2.

ROW 5 P4 (5, 6), *k2, p2, c4L, p2; rep from * 3 times
more, k2, p4 (5, 6).

ROW 6 As row 2.

Rep these last 6 rows until 46 (50, 52) rows have
been worked in cable pattern. Place a removable
marker at each end of next row to mark underarm
and continue in cable pattern until a total of 78 (84,
90) pattern rows have been worked from cast-on
edge.

NEXT ROW Cast off 17 sts, work 16 (18, 20) sts for
back neck and leave on holder, cast off last 17 sts.

FRONT

Left front with buttonband

Cast on 29 (30, 31) sts and knit 6 rows.

Beg cable pattern, starting on a RS row:

ROW I P4 (5, 6), [k2, p2, k4, p2] twice, k5.

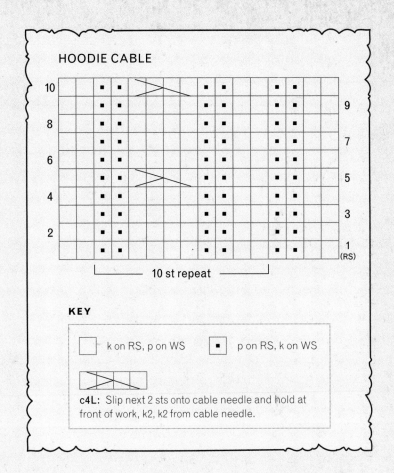

HOODIE CABLE

10 st repeat

KEY

☐ k on RS, p on WS   ■ p on RS, k on WS

c4L: Slip next 2 sts onto cable needle and hold at
front of work, k2, k2 from cable needle.

Row 2 K5, [k2, p4, k2, p2] twice, k4 (5, 6).

Rep rows 1 and 2.

Row 5 P4 (5, 6), [k2, p2, c4L, p2] twice, k5.

Row 6 As row 2.

Rep these 6 rows until 46 (50, 52) rows have been worked. Place a removable marker at beg of next row to mark underarm.

Cont to work in pattern until a total of 69 (73, 79) rows have been worked from cast-on edge.

Next row (ws) Cast off 7 (8, 7) sts, patt to end of row.

Next row Patt to last 2 sts, k2tog.

Next row (0–3 months and 6–9 months) P2tog, patt to end of row. **(9–12 months)** Cast off 2 sts, patt to end of row.

Now dec 1 st at neck edge every RS row 3 (3, 4) times. Work 1 WS row. Cast off all 17 sts.

Right front with buttonhole band

Cast on 29 (30, 31) sts and knit 4 rows.

Next row (1st buttonhole row) K2, yo, k2tog, knit to end of row.

Next row Knit.

Now beg cable pattern.

Row 1 K5, [p2, k4, p2, k2] twice, p4 (5, 6).

Row 2 K4 (5, 6), [p2, k2, p4, k2] twice, k5.

Rep rows 1 and 2.

Row 5 K5, [p2, c4L, p2, k1] twice, p4 (5, 6).

Row 6 As row 2.

Continue to work in pattern as set AND AT THE SAME TIME make buttonholes every 16th (16th, 18th) foll row from previous buttonhole 4 times more. Make the buttonholes in the 5 sts of the buttonhole band, thus:

Buttonhole row (rs) K2, yo, k2tog, k1, patt to end of row.

When 45 (49, 51) rows have been worked, place a removable marker at beg of next row to mark underarm. Cont to work until a total of 68 (72, 78) cable pattern rows have been worked from cast-on edge.

NECK SHAPING

Next row (rs) Cast off 7 (8, 7) sts, patt to end of row.

Next row Patt to last 2 sts, p2tog.

Next row (0–3 months and 6–9 months) K2tog, patt to end of row. **(9–12 months)** Cast off 2 sts, patt to end of row.

Now dec 1 st at neck edge every RS row 3 (3, 4) times. Work 1 row. Cast off 17 sts.

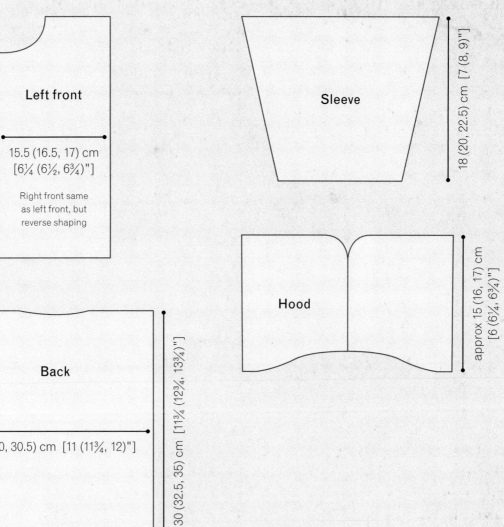

Left front

15.5 (16.5, 17) cm
[6¼ (6½, 6¾)"]

Right front same
as left front, but
reverse shaping

Sleeve

18 (20, 22.5) cm [7 (8, 9)"]

Hood

approx 15 (16, 17) cm
[6 (6¼, 6¾)"]

Back

28 (30, 30.5) cm [11 (11¾, 12)"]

30 (32.5, 35) cm [11¾ (12¾, 13¾)"]

SLEEVES *(make 2 the same)*

Cast on 32 (34, 34) sts. Knit 6 rows.

Beg cable pattern:

Row 1 (1st inc row) Inc in 1st st, k2 (3, 3), p2, [k2, p2, k4, p2] twice, k2, p2, k2 (3, 3), inc in last st.

Row 2 K0 (1, 1), p4, k2, [p2, k2, p4, k2] twice, p2, k2, p4, k0 (1, 1).

Row 3 P0 (1, 1), k4, p2, [k2, p2, k4, p2] twice, k2, p2, k4, p0 (1, 1).

Row 4 As row 2.

Row 5 P0 (1, 1), c4L, p2, [k2, p2, c4L, p2] twice, k2, p2, c4L, p0 (1, 1).

Row 6 As row 2.

These 6 rows set the pattern.

Inc in 1st and last st of next row (Row 7) and then every foll 6th row 5 (5, 7) times more – 46 (48, 52) sts. Work all inc into pattern until 44 sts are on needle. Any further sts should be worked in reverse st st. Once all inc are made, work without shaping until 42 (46, 52) cable pattern rows have been worked from cast-on edge. Cast off.

HOOD AND FINISHING

Weave in loose ends of yarn and block all pieces to size – the cable pattern will stretch out quite a lot. Sew front and back shoulders tog, matching cable patterns.

With RS facing you and starting at right front neck, pick up and knit 14 (16, 18) sts along front neckline, knit 16 (18, 20) across sts on back holder, pick up and knit 14 (16, 18) down left front neckline – 44 (50, 56) sts.

Next row (ws) K3, purl to last 3 sts, k3.

NEXT ROW Knit.

Rep last 2 rows until hood measures 12 (13, 14) cm/ 4¾ (5, 5½)" from neck, ending on a RS row.

NEXT ROW Purl 22 (25, 28) sts, pm, purl rem 22 (25, 28) sts.

DEC ROW (RS) Knit to 2 sts before marker, k2tog, sm, ssk, knit to end of row.

Rep dec row on every RS row 4 times more, ending on a RS row – 34 (40, 46) sts rem.

NEXT ROW With WS facing you, k3, p14 (17, 20) then fold right sides of hood tog (half the hood will be on 1 needle, the other half on the 2nd needle). Taking a 3rd needle, put the tip through 1 st on each of the 2 left needle tips, knitting the 2 sts tog. Rep with the next 2 sts and cast off 1st st. Cont casting off in this way to the end. Weave in yarn tail.

Using mattress st, sew each sleeve onto body between underarm markers, placing centre of sleeve at shoulder seam. Sew side and sleeve seams. Sew on buttons to match buttonholes.

OPTIONAL TASSEL

Cut a rectangle of card the length you want the tassel to be. Wind yarn around the card to the required thickness. Thread a wool needle with a long piece of strong cotton or string, pass it through the top loop and tie it tight. Cut the bottom loop and carefully remove the yarn from the card.

Rethread your needle with yarn and wrap yarn several times around the top of the tassel, about 5 mm (¼") from the looped end. Make a few secure stitches over and through this wrapped yarn. Trim tassel evenly and sew it to the top point of the hood.

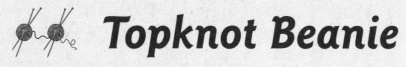

Topknot Beanie

A warm hat is essential for every baby during the cooler months and this beanie is a quick-to-make gift. The crown is knitted in the round using double-pointed needles.

Yarn

- Filatura di Crosa Zarina (100% merino extra-fine; 50 g/1¾ oz; 165 m/180 yd): 1 × ball in #1469 dark-grey (MC); 1 × ball in #1732 sienna orange (A); 1 × ball in #1724 plum (B).

Needles and notions

- 1 × set 2.75 mm (US size 2) dpn OR the size needed to obtain gauge
- markers
- 1 × wool needle

Sizes

- 0–3 months (6–9 months, 9–12 months)

Knitted measurements

- Head circumference: 35 (40, 45) cm/ 13¾ (15¾, 17¾)"
- Lower brim to top of crown: 15 (16, 17) cm/ 6 (6¼, 6¾)"

Gauge

- 24 sts and 32 rows = 10 cm (4") in st st.

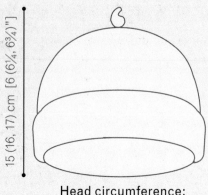

15 (16, 17) cm [6 (6¼, 6¾)"]

Head circumference:
35 (40, 45) cm [13¾ (15¾, 17¾)"]

BRIM

With 2 of the dpn and MC, cast on 16 sts.

Row 1 Knit.

Row 2 Purl.

Rep these 2 rows once more. Cut MC, leaving a short tail for weaving in later.

Begin stripe pattern

Row 1 With A, knit.

Row 2 Knit.

Row 3 Purl.

Row 4 Knit. Cut A.

Row 5 With MC, knit.

Row 6 Purl.

Row 7 Knit.

Row 8 Purl.

Row 9 Knit.

Row 10 Purl. Cut MC.

Row 11 With B, knit.

Row 12 Knit.

Row 13 Purl.

Row 14 Knit. Cut B.

Rows 15–20 As rows 5–10 in MC.

Rep these last 20 rows 5 (6, 7) times more, ending last rep with 4 rows of MC (not 6) – work, slightly stretched, should measure approx 35 (40, 45) cm/ 13¾ (15¾, 17¾)" in length from cast-on edge.

Cast off all sts, leaving a tail of yarn.

Weave in all ends of yarn except the cast-off tail. Using this tail and mattress st, sew the cast-on edge to the cast-off edge, forming a circle.

CROWN

Piping edge

Using B and the set of dpn, and with RS facing you, beg at the seam, pick up and knit 88 (104, 120) sts evenly spaced along the long edge on which the yarn tails have been woven in. Place marker and join into rnd. Knit 5 rounds.

NEXT RND *Sl next st onto right hand needle, pick up corresponding loop at back from 1st B pick-up row (5 rows below), put left tip into front of slipped st (2nd from right hand tip) and through picked-up st and knit both loops tog as 1 st; rep from * until end of rnd. Cut B, leaving a tail.

Join in MC and knit in rnds until piece measures approx 9 cm (3½") from bottom of brim.

NEXT RND *K22 (26, 30), pm; rep from * twice more, knit to end of rnd – 4 sections worked, each with 22 (26, 30) sts.

NEXT RND (DEC RND) *K1, k2tog, knit to last 2 sts

before next marker, ssk, sm; rep from * 3 times more – 8 sts dec.

NEXT RND Knit.

Rep these last 2 rnds until 16 sts rem.

NEXT RND *K1, sl 1, k2tog, psso; rep from * to end – 8 sts rem.

Knit 1 row in MC, then cut yarn leaving a tail.

TOPKNOT AND FINISHING

Join in B and cont to knit the last 8 sts in the rnd for about 35 rows or approx 9 cm (3½"). Cast off all sts. Weave in any ends. Tie topknot into a loose knot. Block beanie lightly over a folded towel or dressmaker's ham.

Sideways Cardigan

This cardigan is knitted in one piece and is quite simple to make. The press studs down the front mean it's easy to get on and off, and it can be worn open or fastened.

Yarn

- Grignasco Bambi (100% merino extra-fine; 50 g/1¾ oz; 225 m/246 yd): 2 × balls in #184 olive (MC); 1 × ball in #191 blue (A); 1 × ball in #680 watermelon (B).

Needles and notions

- 1 × 3 mm (US size 3) circular needle, 80 cm (32") in length OR the size needed to obtain gauge
- 1 × 2.5 mm (US size C/2) crochet hook
- 1 × stitch holder
- 1 × row counter
- 1 × wool needle
- 4 × 11-mm black snap fasteners

Sizes

- 0–3 months (6–9 months, 9–12 months)

Knitted measurements

- Chest: 50 (52, 54) cm/19¾ (20½, 21¼)"
- Length from top of shoulder: 26.5 (28.5, 30.5) cm/10½ (11¼, 12)"
- Sleeve length from underarm: 18 (20.5, 24) cm/ 7 (8, 9½)"

Gauge

- 26 sts and 38 rows = 10 cm (4") in st st.

Note

- The cardigan is knitted sideways, starting at the right cuff and ending at the left cuff. It is knitted on a circular needle but working back and forth.

RIGHT SLEEVE

Begin at right sleeve cuff

In MC, cast on 38 (40, 40) sts.

Beg with a knit row, work 22 (28, 30) rows in st st, without shaping.

Sleeve shaping

NEXT ROW (INC ROW) Inc 1 st at each end of row.

Cont to work in st st, inc 1 st at each end of foll 10th row once, every foll 6th row 3 (3, 4) times, then in every foll 4th row 2 (3, 3) times, every 2nd row 3 (2, 2) times, and every row 2 (4, 8) times – 62 (68, 78) sts.

Increases for front and back

NEXT ROW (WS) Cable cast-on 37 (38, 40) sts.

Purl sts just cast on and purl to end of row.

NEXT ROW Cable cast-on 37 (38, 40) sts. Knit sts just cast on and knit to end of row – 136 (144, 158) sts.

Cont to work without shaping for 30 rows, ending on a RS row.

RIGHT FRONT

Begin front neck shaping

NEXT ROW P68 (72, 79) and slip these sts to holder for back, cast off next 5 (6, 5) sts, purl to end of row.

NEXT ROW Knit.

NEXT ROW Cast off 2 sts at neck edge, purl to end.

Cont to work right front for each size as follows:

0–3 months Dec 1 st at neck edge on foll 5 rows – 56 sts rem.

Purl 1 row.

Begin bottom edge right front curve

Row 1 K2tog, knit to end of row.

Row 2 Purl to last 2 sts, p2tog.

Row 3 Knit.

Row 4 Purl to last 2 sts, p2tog.

Row 5 K2tog, knit to end of row.

Row 6 Purl to last 2 sts, p2tog.

Rows 7 K2tog, knit to end of row.

Row 8 Purl.

Row 9 Cast off 6 sts, knit to end of row.

Cast off all 44 sts.

6–9 months Dec 1 st at neck edge on foll 3 rows, then every second row twice – 59 sts rem.

Purl 1 row.

Begin bottom edge right front curve

Row 1 K2tog, knit to end of row.

Row 2 Purl to last 2 sts, p2tog.

Row 3 Knit.

Row 4 Purl to last 2 sts, p2tog.

Row 5 K2tog, knit to end of row.

Row 6 Purl.

Row 7 Cast off 5 sts, knit to end of row.

Row 8 Purl.

Cast off all 50 sts.

9–12 months Knit next row, then cast off 2 sts at neck edge of next row and purl to end of row. Knit 1 row.

Dec 1 st at neck edge on next 4 rows – 66 sts rem. Purl 1 row.

Begin bottom edge right front curve

Row 1 K2tog, knit to end of row.

Row 2 Purl.

Row 3 Knit.

Row 4 Purl.

Row 5 Knit.

Row 6 Purl to last 2 sts, p2tog.

Row 7 K2tog, knit to end of row.

Row 8 Purl.

Row 9 Cast off 3 sts, knit to end of row.

Row 10 Purl.

Row 11 Cast off 7 sts, knit to end of row.

Cast off all 53 sts.

BACK AND BACK NECK SHAPING

All sizes With RS facing you, rejoin yarn at neck edge and k68 (72, 79) sts from holder.

0–3 months Work 2 rows without shaping. Dec 1 st at neck edge of next row. Work 30 rows without shaping. Inc 1 st at neck edge of next row. Work 2 rows without shaping, ending on a RS row.

6–9 months Work 2 rows without shaping. Dec 1 st at neck edge of next row. Work 32 rows without shaping. Inc 1 st at neck edge of next row. Work 2 rows without shaping, ending on a RS row.

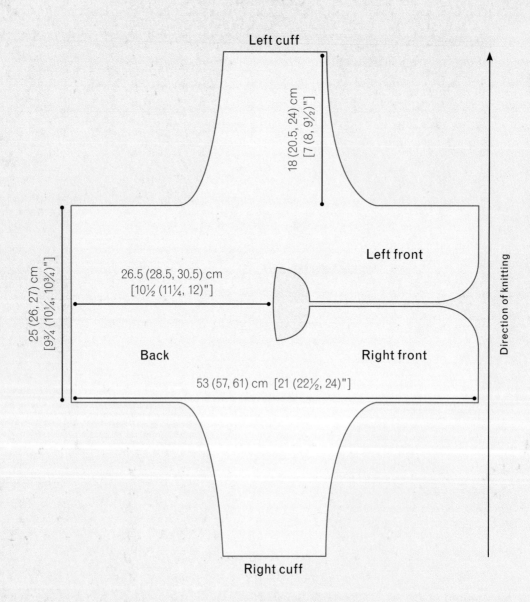

Left cuff

18 (20.5, 24) cm
[7 (8, 9½)"]

Left front

26.5 (28.5, 30.5) cm
[10½ (11¼, 12)"]

25 (26, 27) cm
[9¾ (10¼, 10¾)"]

Back

Right front

53 (57, 61) cm [21 (22½, 24)"]

Direction of knitting

Right cuff

9–12 months Work 3 rows without shaping. Dec
1 st at neck edge of next row. Rep these 4 rows once
more. Now work 28 rows without shaping. Inc 1 st
at neck edge and work 3 rows without shaping.
Rep last 4 rows once more, ending on a RS row.
All sizes Cut yarn, leaving a tail for weaving in
later, and place the sts back onto a stitch holder
for later.

LEFT FRONT

Lower front curve

Cast on 44 (50, 52) sts.

Cont for each size as follows:

0–3 months

Row 1 Purl.

Row 2 Cable cast-on 6 sts and knit all sts
to end of row.

Row 3 Purl.

Row 4 Inc in 1st st, knit to end of row.

Row 5 Purl to last st, inc.

Row 6 Inc in 1st st, knit to end of row.

Row 7 Purl to last st, inc.

Row 8 Knit.

Row 9 Purl to last st, inc.

Row 10 Inc in 1st st, knit to end – 56 sts.

Row 11 Purl.

Row 12 (BEGIN NECK SHAPING) Knit to last st, inc.

Row 13 Inc in 1st st, purl to end of row.

Row 14 Knit to last st, inc.

Row 15 Inc in 1st st, purl to end of row.

Row 16 Knit.

Row 17 Cable cast-on 3 sts, purl all sts to
end of row.

Row 18 Knit.

Row 19 Cable cast-on 5 sts and purl all sts – 68 sts.

6–9 months

Row 1 Purl.

Row 2 Cable cast-on 5 sts, then knit all sts to end of row.

Row 3 Purl.

Row 4 Inc in 1st st, knit to end of row.

Row 5 Purl to last st, inc.

Row 6 Knit.

Row 7 Purl to last st, inc.

Row 8 Inc in 1st st, knit to end of row – 59 sts.

Row 9 Purl.

Row 10 (BEGIN NECK SHAPING) Knit to last st, inc.

Row 11 Purl.

Row 12 Knit to last st, inc.

Row 13 Inc in 1st st, purl to end of row.

Row 14 Knit to last st, inc.

Row 15 Inc in 1st st, purl to end of row.

Row 16 Cable cast-on 2 sts, knit all sts to end of row.

Row 17 Purl.

Row 18 Cable cast-on 6 sts, knit all sts to end of row – 72 sts.

9–12 months

Row 1 Purl.

Row 2 Cable cast-on 7 sts, knit all sts to end of row.

Row 3 Purl.

Row 4 Cable cast-on 3, knit all sts to end of row.

Row 5 Purl.

Row 6 Inc in 1st st, knit to end of row.

Row 7 Purl to last st, inc.

Row 8 Knit.

Row 9 Purl to last st, inc.

Row 10 Knit.

Row 11 Purl.

Row 12 Inc in 1st st, knit to end – 66 sts.

Row 13 Purl.

Row 14 (BEGIN NECK SHAPING) Knit to last st, inc.

Row 15 Inc in 1st st, purl to end of row.

Row 16 Knit to last st, inc.

Row 17 Inc in 1st st, purl to end of row.

Row 18 Knit.

Row 19 Cable cast-on 2 sts, purl all sts to end of row.

Row 20 Knit.

Row 21 Cable cast-on 2 sts, purl all sts to end of row.

Row 22 Knit.

Row 23 Cable cast-on 5 sts, purl all sts to end
of row – 79 sts.

JOINING LEFT FRONT TO BACK
All sizes
NEXT ROW K68 (72, 79) of left front piece, then with
RS facing you and starting from neck edge, knit the
68 (72, 79) sts from holder – 136 (144, 158) sts.
Work 30 rows in st st without shaping.
Cast off 37 (38, 40) sts at beg of next 2 rows – 62 (68,
78) sts rem.

LEFT SLEEVE
Sleeve shaping
Dec 1 st at each end of next 3 (5, 9) rows, then every
2nd row 3 (2, 2) times, every 4th row 2 (3, 3) times,
every 6th row 3 (3, 4) times and 10th row once –
38 (40, 40) sts.
Work 22 (28, 30) rows without shaping.
Cast off all sts.

FINISHING AND EDGING
Block piece to size. Sew underarm and side seams
using mattress stitch. Starting at side seam and
with RS facing you, use crochet hook to work 1 row
of dc right around bottom edge, fronts and neck
in A, then a second row of dc in B.

Work the same 2 rows of dc around each cuff.

Using matching thread, sew snap fasteners in place
down the front of cardigan, starting with one at the
top of the neck and placing the rest approximately
6 cm (2¼") apart.

 # *Frilled Wrap*

With its frilly picot edging, this wrap is delightfully girly. Because it wraps around, the fit will be comfortable for a long time, and it's a breeze to get on and off.

Yarn

- Grignasco Bambi (100% merino extra-fine; 50 g/1¾ oz; 225 m/246 yd): 3 × balls in #670 rose-pink (MC); 1 × ball in #036 dark-red (CC).

Needles and notions

- 1 × 3 mm (US size 3) circular needle, 80 cm (32") in length OR the size needed to obtain gauge
- 2 × 2.5 mm (US size 1 or 2) dpn
- 1 × 2.5 mm (US size C/2) crochet hook
- 3 × stitch holders
- markers
- 1 × row counter
- 1 × wool needle
- 1 × 10 mm button

Sizes

- 0–3 months (6–9 months, 9–12 months)

Knitted measurements

- Chest: 52 (52, 54) cm/20½ (20½, 21¼)"
- Length from top of shoulder: 28.5 (29, 30.5) cm/ 11¼ (11½, 12)"
- Sleeve length from underarm, including frill: 16.5 (19, 20.5) cm/6½ (7½, 8)"

Gauge

- 26 sts and 38 rows = 10 cm (4") in st st using 3 mm circular needle.

Notes

- The wrap is knitted in a single piece to the underarm.
- The large number of sts initially cast on for the frill will rapidly decrease to a more workable number.

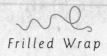

MAIN BODY

Beg at bottom edge and using the circular needle, with CC cast on 705 (705, 733) sts.

Do not join, but work in rows back and forth.

Row 1 Knit.

Break off CC.

Row 2 With MC, purl all sts.

Row 3 K1, p3, *yb, sl 1, k1, psso, k7, k2tog, p3; rep from * to last st, k1.

Row 4 K4, *p9, k3; rep from * to last st, k1.

Row 5 K1, p3, *yb, sl 1, k1, psso, k5, k2tog, p3; rep from * to last st, k1.

Row 6 K4, *p7, k3; rep from * to last st, k1.

Row 7 K1, p3, *yb, sl 1, k1, psso, k3, k2tog, p3; rep from * to last st, k1.

Row 8 K4, *p5, k3; rep from * to last st, k1.

Row 9 K1, p3, *yb, sl 1, k1, psso, k1, k2tog, p3; rep from * to last st, k1.

Row 10 K4, *p3, k3; rep from * to last st, k1.

Row 11 K1, p3, *yb, sl 1, k2tog, psso, p3; rep from * to last st, k1.

Row 12 K4, *p1, k3; rep from * to last st, k1.

Row 13 K1, *p1, k1; rep from * to end of row.

Row 14 K1, *k1, p1; rep from * to last st, k1 – there are now 205 (205, 213) sts on needle.

Row 15 K65 (65, 69), pm, k75, pm, k65 (65, 69).

Row 16 K1, p64 (64, 68), sm, p75, sm, p64 (64, 68), k1.

Row 17 Knit to 1st marker, sm, knit to 2nd marker, sm, knit to end of row.

Row 18 K1, purl to 1st marker, sm, purl to 2nd marker, sm, purl to last st, k1.

Rep rows 17 and 18 twice more.

Row 23 (1ST DEC ROW) Knit to 2 sts before 1st marker, ssk, sm, k2tog, knit to 2 sts before 2nd marker, ssk, sm, k2tog, knit to end of row – 201 (201, 209) sts rem.

Row 24 K1, purl to 1st marker, sm, purl to 2nd marker, sm, purl to last st, k1.

Row 25 Knit to 1st marker, sm, knit to 2nd marker, sm, knit to end of row.

Row 26 K1, purl to 1st marker, sm, purl to 2nd marker, sm, purl to last st, k1.

Rep these last 2 rows 7 times more.

Row 41 (2ND DEC ROW) Knit to 2 sts before 1st marker, ssk, sm, k2tog, knit to 2 sts before 2nd marker, ssk, sm, k2tog, knit to end of row – 197 (197, 205) sts rem.

Row 42 K1, purl to 1st marker, sm, purl to 2nd marker, sm, purl to last st, k1.

Row 43 Knit to 1st marker, sm, knit to 2nd marker, sm, knit to end of row.

Row 44 K1, purl to 1st marker, sm, purl to 2nd marker, sm, purl to last st, k1.

Rep these last 2 rows 1 (1, 2) times more – total of 46 (46, 50) rows worked from cast-on edge.

Begin front neck shaping

Cast off 7 (5, 5) sts at beg of next 2 rows.

Cast off 7 (7, 7) sts at beg of next 2 rows.

Cast off 4 (4, 5) sts at beg of next 2 rows.

Cast off 3 (3, 3) sts at beg of next 2 rows – 155 (159, 165) sts rem.

Next row Cast off 3 (3, 4) sts and knit to 2 sts before 1st marker, ssk, sm, k2tog, knit to 2 sts before 2nd marker, ssk, sm, k2tog, knit to end of row – 148 (152, 157) sts rem.

Next row Cast off 3 (3, 4) sts and purl to end, slipping markers as you come to them – 145 (149, 153) sts rem.

Cont to work in st st, dec 1 st at each end of next 7 (9, 11) rows, ending on a RS row – for **all sizes** there are now 131 sts, placed as follows: 31, marker, 69, marker, 31. Work measures approx 16.5 (17, 18.5) cm/ 6½ (6¾, 7¼)" from cast-on edge.

Next row (ws) Purl to 2 sts before 1st marker, cast off 4 sts (2 either side of marker and remove marker), purl to 2 sts before 2nd marker, cast off 4 sts (2 either side of marker and remove marker), purl to end of row – 123 sts rem.

A total of 64 (66, 72) rows have been worked from cast-on edge.

The back and 2 fronts are now worked separately. Work the right front first, working on the first 29 sts and placing the other sts on stitch holders for later: the centre 65 sts for back on one stitch holder and the last 29 sts for left front on another.

Right front raglan armhole and neck shaping

Dec 1 st at each end of next 12 (11, 11) alt RS rows, then neck edge only of next 4 (6, 7) RS rows – for **all sizes** 1 st remains. Pull up loop and cut yarn to fasten off.

Left front raglan armhole and neck shaping

Sl the 29 sts from holder for the left front onto needle with RS facing you. Complete shaping as for right front, working the decreases on the opposite neck edge to correspond.

Frilled Wrap

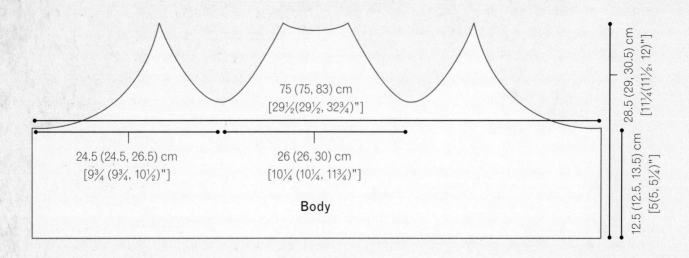

75 (75, 83) cm
[29½(29½, 32¾)"]

28.5 (29, 30.5) cm
[11¼(11½, 12)"]

24.5 (24.5, 26.5) cm
[9¾ (9¾, 10½)"]

26 (26, 30) cm
[10¼ (10¼, 11¾)"]

12.5 (12.5, 13.5) cm
[5(5, 5¼)"]

Body

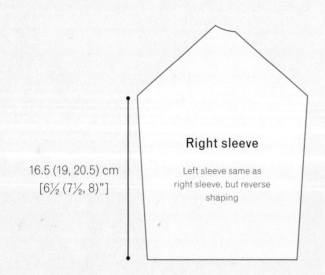

16.5 (19, 20.5) cm
[6½ (7½, 8)"]

Right sleeve

Left sleeve same as
right sleeve, but reverse
shaping

Back

Sl the 65 sts for the back onto needle. Beg with RS facing you and dec 1 st at each end of every RS row until 25 sts rem. Place sts on holder for neckband.

RIGHT SLEEVE
All sizes

With CC and using circular needle, cast on 157 sts. Do not join, but work in rows back and forth.

Row 1 Knit.

Break off yarn, leaving a tail for sewing border later.

Row 2 With MC, purl.

Row 3 P3, *yb, sl 1, k1, psso, k7, k2tog, p3; rep from * to end of row.

Row 4 K3, *p9, k3; rep from * to end of row.

Row 5 P3, *yb, sl 1, k1, psso, k5, k2tog, p3; rep from * to end of row.

Row 6 K3, *p7, k3; rep from * to end of row.

Row 7 P3, *yb, sl 1, k1, psso, k3, k2tog, p3; rep from * to end of row.

Row 8 K3, *p5, k3; rep from * to end of row.

Row 9 P3, *yb, sl 1, k1, psso, k1, k2tog, p3; rep from * to end of row.

Row 10 K3, *p3, k3; rep from * to end of row.

Row 11 P3, *yb, sl 1, k2tog, psso, p3; rep from * to end of row.

Row 12 K3, *p1, k3; rep from * to end of row.

Row 13 P1, *k1, p1; rep from * to end of row.

Row 14 *K1, p1; rep from * to last st, k1 – there are now 47 sts on needles.

Work 10 rows in st st without shaping.

NEXT ROW (INC ROW) Inc 1 st at each end of row and then every foll 8th (6th, 6th) row 4 (6, 8) times more – 57 (61, 65) sts.

Cont in st st without shaping until work measures approx 16.5 (19, 20.5) cm/6½ (7½, 8)" from cast-on edge, ending on a WS row.

Raglan armhole shaping
All sizes

Row 1 K2tog, knit to last 2 sts, k2tog.

Row 2 P2tog, purl to last 2 sts, p2tog.

Rep these 2 rows until 11 sts rem, ending on a WS row.

Sleeve cap

NEXT ROW Cast off 6 sts, knit next 2 sts, k2tog – 4 sts rem.

Row 2 K2tog, knit to last 2 sts, k2tog.

Rep these 2 rows until 11 sts rem, ending on a RS row.

Sleeve cap

NEXT ROW Cast off 6 sts, purl next 2 sts, p2tog –
4 sts rem.

NEXT ROW K2tog twice – 2 sts rem.

NEXT ROW P2tog, pull loop up and cut yarn to
fasten off, leaving a tail of yarn long enough to sew
the sleeve onto the body.

FINISHING

Weave in all loose ends except one CC tail from
each cuff – these will be used to sew cuff border
tog. Lightly block all pieces (do not press frills).
Sew up sleeve seams, sewing the CC borders tog
using the CC tail not woven in. Using mattress
st, sew raglan sleeves into armholes, placing the
underarm seam to the centre of the 4 cast-off sts
of body and making sure the higher part of the
armholes are stitched to the body back and the
lower to the fronts. Sew as close as possible to the
sts on the stitch holder at back of neck.

NEXT ROW P2tog twice – 2 sts rem.

NEXT ROW K2tog, pull loop up and cut yarn to
fasten off, leaving a tail of yarn long enough to sew
the sleeve onto the body.

LEFT SLEEVE

Work as for right sleeve until work measures approx
16.5 (19, 20.5) cm/6½ (7½, 8)" from cast-on edge,
ending on a RS row.

Raglan armhole shaping

All sizes

Row 1 P2tog, purl to last 2 sts, p2tog.

Neckband

Using MC, and with RS of work facing you, start at the beg of the right hand front neck shaping, and pick up and knit 48 (50, 54) sts along front edge, 6 sts across top of sleeve to back neck, then knit across 25 sts on holder, then knit 6 sts across top of left sleeve and 48 (50, 54) sts down left hand front to edge – 133 (137, 145) sts. As you pick up sts, try to cover any gaps by knitting 2 loops tog or passing 1 picked-up st over another. Any gaps left can be stitched over at the back once the neckband is complete.

Purl 1 row.

Break off MC.

NEXT ROW With CC, knit 1 row.

Make crochet picot border

Cast off pwise. Don't break yarn at last st, but insert crochet hook into loop and work a row of picot around complete neckline, as follows:

Ch3, sl st into 3rd ch from hook, *miss 1 loop of a cast-off st, 1dc into next st, ch3, sl st into 3rd ch from hook; rep from * to end. End with a dc and fasten with a sl st to cast off edge. Break yarn and fasten off.

Lower edging

Using CC, and with RS of work facing you, start at the lower left hand front. Insert crochet hook into 1st st and work a row of picot right around lower edge, ending at bottom right front, as follows:

Ch3, sl st into 3rd ch from hook, *miss 1 loop of a cast-off st, 1dc into next st, ch3, sl st into 3rd ch from hook; rep from * to end. End with a dc and fasten with a sl st to cast off edge. Break yarn and fasten off.

Cuff edging

Using CC, and with RS of sleeve facing you, insert crochet hook into a st at seam and crochet 1 row of picot as for lower edging.

Buttonhole tab

With MC and dpn, cast on 20 sts.

Knit 1 row.

NEXT ROW K3, [yf, k2tog, k2] 3 times, knit to end – 3 buttonholes made.

NEXT ROW Knit (working yos from previous row as new sts).

Cast off all 17 sts.

Ties (make 2)

With MC and 2 dpn, cast on 3 sts, leaving a tail long enough to sew the tie onto the garment later. Knit 1st row, then without turning the work, push sts to the right hand end of the needle, and knit with the other needle, pulling the yarn from behind. Cont knitting in this way until the tie is 18 cm (7") long. Cut yarn, leaving a tail. Thread the tail through a wool needle and draw the threaded needle through the 3 sts on the knitting needle, pulling tightly as you drop them off the needle. Now use 1 or 2 sts to fasten firmly, thread the yarn down into the cord as far as you can and cut yarn.

Attaching fastenings

Sew button onto the RS of the end of neckband of the left front.

Place wrap on a flat surface with the back RS down. Fold the left front with the button (facing you it will be on your right hand side) to your left, making sure the increases at the side form a 'side seam'. Keep the front hem level with the back hem.

Now fold the right side of wrap (it will be on your left) over the other front – it will be on top and to your right – making sure the side increases are forming a 'side seam' and the hems are level.

One tie will be sewn onto the end of this neckband (the right hand front) that is on the top and the other tie will be sewn at the 'side seam' at the same level. Mark the side seam position and sew both ties in position. Use the cast-on tail of the ties to sew them on. Tie into a bow, then turn the wrap inside out.

Lay out the wrap flat with the back WS down so the sides are straight and hems level. Attach the buttonhole tab to the armhole seam – about 2 cm (¾") up from the centre underarm 'side seam' – so the buttonholes are angled to fasten onto the button.

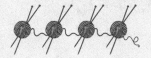 # *Stroller Blanket*

This small blanket is so versatile – tuck it around baby in the stroller on chilly days, use it as a play mat, or simply drape it over a chair in the nursery as a gorgeous decoration.

Yarn

- Sublime (cashmere/merino/silk dk; 50 g/1¾ oz; 116m/127 yd): 4 × balls in # 0055 Boater/blue (MC); 4 × balls in #0052 Tease/pink (CC).

Needles and notions

- 3 × 4 mm (US size 6) circular needles, each 80 cm (32") in length OR the size needed to obtain gauge.

Knitted measurements

- Approx 45 cm × 70 cm (17¾" × 27½"), including a 9 cm (3½") border.

Gauge

- 17 sts and 36 rounds = 10 cm (4") in garter st.
- 20 sts and 28 rounds = 10 cm (4") in st st.

Notes

- The centre section is worked on a circular needle back and forth. It is made up of 5 panels, each separated by a horizontal band of knit or purl rows.

- The border is worked in the round using 3 circular needles. Sts picked up from 1 long side of blanket are on 1 needle and sts picked up from 1 short side of blanket are on a 2nd needle. The 3rd needle is the working needle.

- A mitred right angle is formed at each corner, where markers will be placed.

- Garter stitch, in the rnd, is worked as 1 rnd knit, 1 rnd purl.

CENTRE SECTION

Work on 1 circular needle back and forth. Do not join into a round. With MC and using the thumb method cast on 128 sts.

BAND Knit 3 rows.

Panel 1

Row 1 (ws) K1, *k1, p1, k2, p1; rep from * to last 2 sts, k2.

Row 2 P1, *p1, yb, sl 1 pwise, yf, p1; rep from * to last 4 sts, p1, yb, sl 1 pwise, yf, p2.

Row 3 K1, *k1, p1, k2, p1; rep from * to last 2 sts; k2.

Rep these last 2 rows 13 times more, ending on WS.

BAND Knit 5 rows, ending with a RS row.

Panel 2

Row 1 (ws) *P1 tbl, k5; rep from * to last 2 sts, p1 tbl, k1.

Row 2 *P1, k1 tbl, p1, k3; rep from * to last 2 sts, p1, k1 tbl.

Rep these last 2 rows 10 times more and then rep row 1 once more. There are now 11 ridge rows on RS of Panel 2 and last row worked was on WS.

BAND Starting with a RS row, purl 4 rows.

Panel 3

Row 1 (RS) P1, *k3, p11; rep from * until 1 st rem, k1.

Row 2 *K11, p3; rep from * to last 2 sts, k2.

Row 3 P3, *k3, p11; rep from * to end of row, ending last rep p10.

Row 4 K9, *p3, k11; rep from * to end of row, ending last rep k4.

Row 5 P5, *k3, p11; rep from * to end of row, ending last rep p8.

Row 6 K7, *p2, k11; rep from * to end of row, ending last rep k6.

Row 7 P7, *k3, p11; rep from * to end of row, ending last rep p6.

Row 8 K5, *p3, k11; rep from * to end of row, ending last rep k8.

Row 9 P9, *k3, p11; rep from * to end of row, ending last rep p4.

Row 10 K3, *p3, k11; rep from * to end of row, ending last rep k10.

Row 11 P11, *k3, p11; rep from * to end of row, ending last rep p2.

Row 12 K1, *p3, k11; rep from * until 1 st rem, k1.

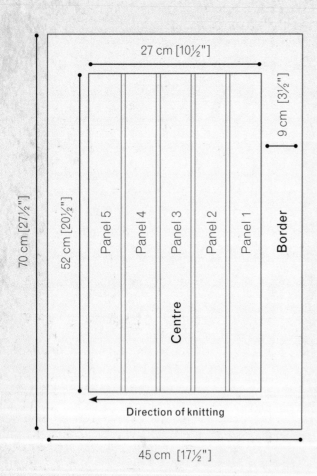

Direction of knitting

27 cm [10½"]

9 cm [3½"]

Border

Panel 1
Panel 2
Panel 3
Panel 4
Panel 5

Centre

52 cm [20½"]

70 cm [27½"]

45 cm [17½"]

Row 13 As row 11.
Row 14 As row 10.
Row 15 As row 9.
Row 16 As row 8.
Row 17 As row 7.
Row 18 As row 6.
Row 19 As row 5.
Row 20 As row 4.
Row 21 As row 3.
Row 22 As row 2.
Row 23 As row 1.

Band Beg with a WS row, purl 5 rows.

Panel 4
Row 1 (RS) K1, *yf, sl 1 pwise and leaving yarn in front of work, k1 (creating a yo); rep from * to end of row, ending with sl 1 pwise.
Row 2 *Knit yo and next st tog, p1; rep from * to end of row.
Note: The 1st st of row 2 will be a slipped st and the yarn will be hanging at back of work from the 2nd st. To knit this 1st st, insert tip of right hand needle into the front of loop (the slipped st from previous row) as if ready to knit. Now wrap the yarn from the back,

right around both needles once, then bring it from behind through the 2 strands and knit them tog.

Rep rows 1 and 2 until 10 rows have been worked.

NEXT ROW *K1, p1; rep to end of row.

Knit 3 rows.

Rep rows 1 and 2 another 5 times.

BAND Knit 5 rows, ending with a RS row.

Panel 5

SET-UP ROW *P1, k3; rep from * to end of row.

ROW 1 (RS) P3, *k1 wrapping yarn twice around needle, p3, k1, p3; rep from * until 5 sts rem, k1 wrapping yarn twice around needle, p3, k1.

ROW 2 *P1, k3, yf, sl 1 dropping extra loop, yb, k3; rep from * to end of row.

ROW 3 P3, *yb, sl 1, yf, p3, k1, p3; rep from * until last 5 sts, yb, sl 1, yf, p3, k1.

ROW 4 *P1, k3, yf, sl 1, yb, k3; rep from * to end of row.

Rep these last 4 rows 4 times more – 20 rows total.

BAND Knit 4 rows, then cast off all sts loosely.

BORDER

Mark sides into equal divisions with markers or small safety pins, to help you pick up sts evenly. With RS of blanket facing you, and using CC and one of the circular needles, start at the far right hand side of one of the long sides and pick up and knit 128 sts (this should be fairly easy as you will be picking up either cast-on or cast-off sts). Place a marker before the last st picked up. (Make sure the last st picked up is at the very end of the row as it will become the corner st.) After this last st picked up, place a 2nd marker, then pick up and knit

88 sts evenly along the 1st short side, placing a 3rd marker before the last st picked up (2nd corner st). Push these sts away from the ends of the needle to prevent them falling off as you are working on the 2nd needle.

With the 2nd circular needle, continue to pick up and knit sts in the same way – 128 sts along the 2nd long side, placing a marker before and after last st worked (3rd corner), then pick up 88 more sts along last (short) side, placing a marker before last st worked (4th corner) – 432 sts worked. The 1st and 2nd needles act as the 4th and 8th markers.

RND 1 With working needle in right hand, m1 (lift yarn lying between the st just worked and the next st and place it on the left hand needle, then knit into back of this loop), knit to 1st marker, m1, sm, k1, sm, m1, knit to next marker, m1, sm, k1 (this completes sts on 1st needle – half the round). All the sts from the left hand needle are now on the right hand (working) needle. Push the sts down from the needle tips to prevent them falling off. Use the new working needle to rep the 2nd half of the rnd exactly as the 1st half, making sure the yarn is held firmly when joining in a new needle to prevent gaps in sts. Once the rnd is completed, you have 4 single corner sts between markers and you have made 1 new st either side of the corner st. In rnd 1 you have increased 8 sts.

RND 2 Purl all sts, slipping markers as you come to them.

Rep these 2 rnds, increasing 8 sts each rep, until border measures approx 9 cm (3½").

Knit rnd 1 once more. Cast off loosely pwise on a purl round.

Weave in all ends neatly.

 # *Preppy Cardigan*

Cardigans are so easy to get on and off, and the large v-neck of this design makes it even easier –
you can choose whether to unbutton it, or simply lift it off over baby's head.

Yarn

- Araucania Ranco Solid (75% wool/25% polyamide; 100 g/3½ oz; 344 m/376 yd): 2 × hanks in teal (MC).

- Filatura di Crosa Zarina (100% merino extra-fine; 50 g/1¾ oz; 165 m/180 yd): 1 × ball in #1732 sienna orange (CC).

Needles and notions

- 1 × pair 3 mm (US size 3) needles OR the size needed to obtain gauge

- stitch holders

- small safety pins for holding a small number of stitches and pinning neckband

- markers

- 1 × row counter

- 1 × wool needle

- 5 (6, 6) × 12 mm buttons

Sizes

- 0–3 months (6–9 months, 9–12 months)

Knitted measurements

- Chest: 51 (54, 56) cm/20 (21¼, 22)"

- Length from top of shoulder: 26.5 (28.5, 30.5) cm/ 10½ (11¼, 12)"

- Sleeve length from underarm: 17 (19, 22) cm/ 6¾ (7½, 8¾)"

Gauge

- 25 sts and 32 rows = 10 cm (4") in st st.

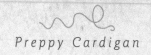
BACK

With MC, cast on 63 (67, 69) sts.

Row 1 *K1, p1; rep from * to last st, k1.

Row 2 *P1, k1; rep from * to last st, p1.

Row 3 *K1, p1; rep from * to last st, k1.

Cut MC, leaving a tail to weave in later.

Row 4 With CC, *p1, k1; rep from * to last st, p1.
Break off CC.

Row 5 With MC, as row 1.

Row 6 As row 2.

Next row (RS) P1 (2, 4), *k1, p4; rep from * to last
2 (3, 5) sts, k1, p1 (2, 4).

Next row K1 (2, 4), *p1, k4; rep from * to last
2 (3, 5) sts, p1, k1 (2, 4).

Rep last 2 rows until work measures 16 (17, 18.5) cm/
6¼ (6¾, 7¼)" from cast-on edge, ending on a WS –
50 (52, 58) rows worked from cast-on edge.

Raglan armhole shaping

Next row (RS) P1, ssk, patt to last 3 sts,
k2tog, p1.

Next row K1, p1, patt to last 2 sts, p1, k1.

Rep these last 2 rows until 31 (33, 33) sts rem,
ending on a WS. Cast off.

LEFT FRONT (*Buttonband side*)

With MC, cast on 37 (39, 41) sts.

Row 1 (RS) *K1, p1; rep from * to last st, k1.

Row 2 *P1, k1; rep from * to last st, p1.

Row 3 As row 1.

Row 4 With MC, [p1, k1] twice, with CC *p1, k1; rep
from * to end of row. Break off both yarns leaving tails
to weave in later. Rejoin MC to continue at row 5.

Row 5 Using MC, *k1, p1; rep from * to last 5 sts, k1
with CC, then [p1, k1] twice in MC. These last
4 sts will be above the 4 MC sts from previous row.

Row 6 [P1, k1] twice in MC yarn, p1 in CC, *k1, p1;
rep from * to end of row in MC. Inc 1 st at end of this
row for **0–3 months** only – 38 (39, 41) sts.

The 7 rib sts with the single CC stitch will be the
front buttonband.

Next row (RS) P1 (2, 4), *k1, p4; rep from * to
last 7 sts, k1, p1, with MC yb, with CC k1, with MC yf,
[p1, k1] twice.

Next row With MC [p1, k1] twice, yf, with CC p1,
with MC yb, with MC k1, p1, *k4, p1; rep from * to
last 1 (2, 4) sts, p1 (2, 4).

Note: As you knit this CC st: on a RS row, hold the
MC across the CC st at the back of work, then pick
up the CC yarn and knit the st, trapping the MC
under the CC. On a WS row, move the MC yarn to
the front (the side facing you), cross it over the CC
yarn and hold it to the left, pick up the CC yarn and
purl the st, then move the MC yarn to the back of
work (which is actually the front of the buttonband),
and knit the next st with MC.

Rep these last 2 rows, keeping the single CC st in the
band, until work measures 16 (17, 18.5) cm/6¼ (6¾,
7¼)" from cast-on edge, ending on a WS row – 50 (52,
58) rows from beg of piece.

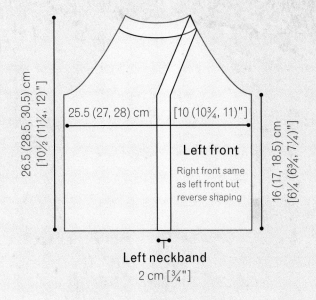

26.5 (28.5, 30.5) cm [10½ (11¼, 12)"]

25.5 (27, 28) cm [10 (10¾, 11)"]

16 (17, 18.5) cm [6¼ (6¾, 7¼)"]

Left front

Right front same
as left front but
reverse shaping

Left neckband

2 cm [¾"]

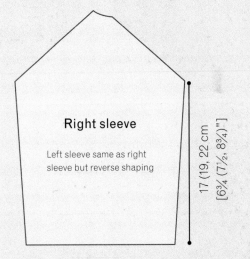

Right sleeve

Left sleeve same as right
sleeve but reverse shaping

17 (19, 22 cm [6¾ (7½, 8¾)"]

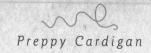

Special Instructions

MAKE BUTTONHOLES IN BAND STS

On a RS row:

Row 1 With MC, k1, p1, k1, yf, put right hand needle into front of next 2 sts (the 2nd st is the CC st) as if to knit and take MC over the top of the needle to make a yo. Now holding down MC at back of work, bring the CC over it to knit the 2 sts tog in CC. Next, hold down CC at back of work and bring MC over it to the front between the needles and p1, k1 in MC.

Row 2 With MC p1, k1, yf. Hold down MC and bringing CC over MC, p1 in CC. Now hold down CC and bringing MC over CC and between needles, knit into back of yo loop from previous row. With MC p1, k1, p1.

On a WS row:

Row 1 With MC, p1, k1, yf. Hold down MC, bring CC over it and with CC p2tog. Hold down CC and make a MC yo by bringing MC right around needle. MC is now at front of work between needles. With MC p1, k1, p1.

Row 2 With MC k1, p1, k1, p tbl of yo. Take MC to back of work and holding it down, bring CC over it and k1. Holding down CC at back of work, bring MC forward between needles and p1, k1.

Raglan armhole shaping

NEXT ROW (RS) Cast off 2 sts, patt to end of row.

NEXT ROW Patt to last 2 sts, p1, k1.

NEXT ROW (DEC ROW) P1, ssk, patt to end of row.

NEXT ROW Patt to last 2 sts, p1, k1.

Rep the last 2 rows until 57 (59, 63) rows have been worked from cast-on edge – 33 (34, 37) sts rem.

NEXT ROW (WS) Patt the 7 band sts then slip them onto a large safety pin or small stitch holder. (Don't cut the CC yarn, instead wind a small ball that will be used to complete the band and will prevent having a join. Keep the ball attached to band with a large safety pin or clip.) K2tog, patt to last 2 sts, p1, k1.

NEXT ROW (ARMHOLE EDGE) P1, ssk, patt to end of row.

NEXT ROW K2tog, patt to end of row.

Rep the last 2 rows until 3 sts rem.

NEXT ROW P2, k1.

NEXT ROW P1, ssk.

NEXT ROW P2tog.

Pull loop up and break off yarn.

RIGHT FRONT (Buttonhole band side)

(see Special Instructions: Make Buttonholes in Band Sts)

With MC, cast on 37 (39, 41) sts.

ROW 1 (RS) *K1, p1; rep from * to last st, k1.

ROW 2 *P1, k1; rep from * to last st, p1.

ROW 3 K1, p1, k1, yf, k2tog, p1, *k1, p1; rep from * to last st, k1. Break off MC.

ROW 4 With CC, *p1, k1; rep from * until 4 sts rem (including the yo of previous row), with MC knit through back of yo, p1, k1, p1.

ROW 5 With MC [k1, p1] twice, with CC k1, with MC *p1, k1; rep from * to last st, k1.

ROW 6 With MC *p1, k1; rep from * until 5 sts rem, with CC, p1, with MC [k1, p1] twice. Inc 1 st at beg of this row for **0–3 months only** – 38 (39, 41) sts.

The 7 rib sts with the single CC st will be the front buttonhole band.

Note: When knitting the single CC st in the front band, always keep the MC yarn in back of work and trap yarn under the CC as the contrast st is worked.

NEXT ROW (RS) With MC, [k1, p1] twice, with CC k1, with MC, p1, k1, *p4, k1; rep from * until 1 (2, 4) sts rem, p1 (2, 4).

NEXT ROW K1 (2, 4), *p1, k4; rep from * until 7 sts rem; p1, k1, with CC, p1; with MC [k1, p1] twice.

Rep these last 2 rows, keeping the single CC st in the band, AND AT THE SAME TIME make buttonholes on foll rows.

Buttonhole rows

The 1st buttonhole was in row 3.

0–3 months Make a buttonhole every foll 13th row 4 times more. (Last buttonhole is worked on row 55.)

6–9 months Make a buttonhole every foll 11th row 5 times more. (Last buttonhole is worked on row 58.)

9–12 months Make a buttonhole every foll 12th row 5 times more. (Last buttonhole is worked on row 63.)

When 51 (53, 59) rows have been worked from cast-on edge – 16 (17, 18.5) cm / 6¼ (6¾, 7¼)" from cast-on edge – commence the raglan armhole shaping. Continue to make buttons as set.

Raglan armhole shaping

NEXT ROW (WS) Cast off 2 sts, patt to end of row.

NEXT ROW (DEC ROW) Patt to last 3 sts, k2tog, p1.

NEXT ROW K1, p1, patt to end of row.

Rep the last 2 rows until 58 (60, 64) rows have been worked from cast-on edge – 33 (34, 37) sts rem.

NEXT ROW (RS) Patt the 7 band sts then slip them onto a large safety pin or small stitch holder.(Don't cut the CC yarn, but instead wind a small ball that will be used to complete the band and will prevent having a join. Keep the ball attached to band with a large safety pin or clip.) Patt to last 3 sts, k2tog, p1.

NEXT ROW (ARMHOLE EDGE) K1, p1, patt to last 2 sts, k2tog.

NEXT ROW Patt to last 3 sts, k2tog, p1.

Rep the last 2 rows until 3 sts rem.

NEXT ROW (WS) K1, p2tog.

NEXT ROW K2tog, pull up loop and break off yarn.

RIGHT SLEEVE

With MC, cast on 43 (45, 47) sts.

Row 1 *K1, p1; rep from * to last st, k1.

Row 2 *P1, k1; rep from * to last st, p1.

Row 3 As row 1.

Row 4 As row 2 in CC.

Row 5 As row 1 in MC.

Row 6 As row 2 in MC

NEXT ROW (RS) P1 (2, 3), *k1, p4; rep from * to last 2 (3, 4) sts, k1, p1 (2, 3).

NEXT ROW K1 (2, 3), *p1, k4; rep from * to last 2 (3, 4) sts, k1, p1 (2, 3).

NEXT ROW (1ST INC ROW) Inc in 1st and last st – 45 (47, 49) sts. Work all increases into patt.

Now inc in every foll 6th row until there are 57 (63, 67) sts – 45 (57, 63) rows have been worked from cast-on edge. Cont without shaping until work measures 17 (19, 21.5) cm/6¾ (7½, 8½)" from cast-on edge, ending on a WS row – approx 54 (60, 68) rows worked from cast-on edge.

Raglan armhole shaping

Cast off 3 sts at beg of next 2 rows.
DEC ROW P1, ssk, patt to last 3 sts, k2tog, p1.
NEXT ROW K1, p1, patt to last 2 sts, p1, k1.
Rep these last 2 rows until 17 (17, 19) sts rem, ending on a WS row – 86 (98, 108) rows worked from cast-on edge.

Sleeve cap

NEXT ROW Cast off 10 sts, patt to last 3 sts, k2tog, p1.
NEXT ROW K1, p1, patt to end of row.
NEXT ROW K2tog, patt to last 3 sts, k2tog, p1.
NEXT ROW K1, p1, patt to end of row.
Cast off rem 4 (4, 6) sts.

LEFT SLEEVE

Knit as for right sleeve until raglan armhole shaping is complete – 17 (17, 19) sts.

Sleeve cap

NEXT ROW P1, ssk, patt to end of row.
NEXT ROW (WS) Cast off 10 sts, patt to last 2 sts, p1, k1.
NEXT ROW P1, ssk, patt to last 2 sts, k2tog.
NEXT ROW Patt to last 2 sts, p1, k1.
Cast off rem 4 (4, 6) sts.

COMPLETING BAND

Using mattress st and picking up the edge sts of each piece, sew the raglan sleeves in place. Make sure the higher side of each raglan sleeve is at the back.

Bands

Mark centre back of neck on back piece with a safety pin.

Rejoin MC at inside edge of buttonband, with RS facing you, inc in 1st st (this increase is an edge st and will be used to stitch the band onto front body – knit this st on every row). Knit the 7 band sts as set, using the small CC ball that you wound off before for the stripe. As you knit, pin the band in position along the garment edge. Slightly stretch the band,

Special Instructions

GRAFT NECKBAND

STEP 1 Sl the knit sts off one side of neckband onto a needle and the purl sts onto a holder.

STEP 2 Rep with the other side.

STEP 3 Hold the 2 knitting needles with the knit sts on them WS facing together in your left hand. Thread the wool needle with a yarn tail from one of the knitted bands and hold it in your right hand.

STEP 4 Pass wool needle through the 1st st on the front knitting needle as if to knit and slip it off the knitting needle.

STEP 5 Pass wool needle through the 2nd st on the front knitting needle as if to purl but leave the st on the knitting needle.

STEP 6 Pass wool needle through the 1st st on the back knitting needle as if to purl and slip it off the knitting needle.

STEP 7 Pass wool needle through the 2nd st on the back knitting needle as if to knit and leave the st on the knitting needle.

Rep steps 4 to 7 until all sts are joined.

STEP 8 Turn work, transfer rem sts from each holder onto the 2 needles and rep steps 3 to 7.

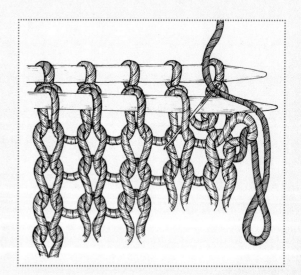

keeping the body unstretched. Once the band seems to have reached the centre back, leave the band sts on a stitch holder, cut both yarns, leaving a long tail of each colour. Make last knitted row finish at outside edge of band (i.e. not the edge that will be stitched to the back neck).

Rep this with the buttonhole band, but beg with WS facing you, making the inc st at the inside edge of band.

Now sew each band to garment. Starting at the front V, and using mattress stitch, catch the edge st of the band as you work. Sew bands to about 2 cm (¾") short of centre back of neck and leave yarn tails to complete sewing later. If bands are too long, undo rows until they match at centre back – if too short, knit more rows.

Now graft the 8 sts tog using the MC yarn from the knitted band (*see Special Instructions: Graft Neckband*): place the 4 knit sts of each side of band on 2 needles; place the purl sts on holders. Graft the knit sts, then turn work and graft the purl sts

(which when turned will be knit sts). Sew band across centre back of neck.

FINISHING

Weave in all other ends and neaten any gaps in the grafting. Match side and sleeve seams and sew using mattress st. Sew buttons on left band to line up with buttonholes.

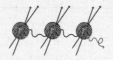 # Long Socks

These socks are perfect for keeping toes toasty and warm – and because they're long they can't easily be kicked off! (There are also instructions for making a shorter version if you prefer.)

Yarn

- Grignasco Bambi (100% merino extra-fine; 50 g/1¾ oz; 225 m/246 yd): 1 × ball in main colour (MC). (Note that 1 ball will make 2 pairs of socks.) Colours used here include: #166 dark-burgundy, #183 dark-olive, #070 navy, #002 black. 3 × balls in different contrast colours (A, B and C) (about 10 m/11yd of each). Colours used here include #036 dark-red, #167 purple, #168 fuchsia, #184 olive, #185 light-green, #193 turquoise, #239 aqua, #671 hot-pink, #680 watermelon.

Needles and notions

- 1 × set 2.25 mm (US size 1) dpn OR the size needed to obtain gauge

- markers

- 1 × wool needle

Sizes

- 0–3 months (6–9 months, 9–12 months)

Knitted measurements

- Back of heel to tip of toe (approx): 8.5 (10.5, 12) cm/ 3¼ (4¼, 4¾)"

- Foot circumference: 12 cm (4¾")

- Long sock from top of sock to bottom of heel: 13 cm (5")

- Short sock (variation) from top of sock to bottom of heel: 11.5 cm (4¼")

Gauge

- 30 sts and 40 rnds = 10 cm (4") in st st worked in the rnd.

Notes

- When not working ssk, ssp and sssp decreases, sl all other sts pwise.

- Using the instructions, make 2 socks the same.

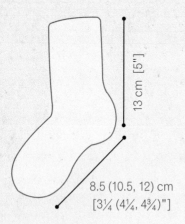

13 cm [5"]

8.5 (10.5, 12) cm
[3¼ (4¼, 4¾)"]

TOP OF SOCK

Using MC, cast on 36 sts using thumb method
and join into a round.

Rnd 1 *K1, p1; rep from * to end of rnd. Place
marker between last 2 sts so it doesn't fall off
needle.

Rep this rnd 5 times more – 6 rows of k1, p1 rib.

Knit 4 rnds.

Begin stripe pattern

Rnd 1 Using A and leaving MC at back of work, k1,
*sl 1, k2; rep from * to end of rnd.

Rnd 2 Still with A, yf, p1, * yb, sl 1 pwise, yf, p2; rep
from * to end of rnd.

Rnd 3 Using MC, knit.

Rnd 4 Using MC, knit.

Cut A leaving a tail to weave in later.

Rnds 5–8 Rep rnds 1 to 4, using B instead of A.

Rnds 9–12 Rep rnds 1 to 4, using C instead of A.

Rnds 13–16 Using MC, knit.

Rep rnds 1–16 twice more for long sock, or once
more for short sock.

When the last rep has been worked, knit another
2 rnds in MC. The work should measure about
11 cm (4¼") from cast-on edge for the long sock,
or 8 cm (3") for the short sock.

HEEL

Knit next rnd until 9 sts rem on last needle. Arrange
sts so there are 18 sts on the 1st needle for heel
(remove marker; yarn will be on the right hand side
of these sts), and 9 sts on each of the 2nd and 3rd
needles for instep to be worked later. The 18 sts for
heel are worked in short rows as follows:

Row 1 (RS) K17, turn (there will be 1 st unworked
on left needle).

Row 2 Yo backwards, p16, turn (1 st unworked).

Row 3 Yo as usual, k15 sts to the pair of sts made
by the yo of previous row leaving 3 sts on left needle

(i.e. yo loop from previous row and 1 pair sts) – do not work these. Turn.

Row 4 Yo backwards, p14 sts to paired sts made by the previous row, turn.

Row 5 Yo as usual, k13 sts to paired sts made by the previous row, turn.

Row 6 Yo backwards, p12 sts to paired sts made by the previous row, turn.

Row 7 Yo as usual, k11 sts to paired sts made by the previous row, turn.

Row 8 Yo backwards, p10 sts to paired sts made by the previous row, turn.

Row 9 Yo as usual, k9 sts to paired sts made by the previous row, do not turn.

There will be 8 unpaired sts between the yos. This will end on a RS row and you cont without turning to make the heel base as follows:

Row 1 K1 (the 1st st of the 1st pair on the left hand needle), slip the next st (the yo which was paired with the st just knitted) pwise, then insert the left hand needle into the slipped st from front to back and slip the st back onto the left hand needle (this has just corrected the mount of the st), k2tog (the yo with the 1st st of the next pair, leaving a yo as the 1st st on the left needle), turn.

Row 2 (ws) Yo backwards, purl to paired st made by yo of previous row, purl the 1st st of the pair, ssp (the yo with the 1st st of the next pair, leaving a yo as the 1st st on the left needle), turn.

Row 3 Yo, knit to the paired st made by yo of previous row, knit the 1st st of the pair (the next 2 loops will be yos), correct the mount of each of these 2 yos (as described in row 1), k3tog (2 yos with the 1st st of the next pair), turn.

Row 4 Yo backwards, purl to next yo (the next 2 loops are yos), sssp (2 yos with the 1st st of the next pair), turn.

Row 5 Yo, knit to next yo (the next 2 loops will be yos), correct the mount of each of these yos, k3tog (2 yos with the 1st st of the next pair), turn.

Rep the last 2 rows until all the yos of the heel have been worked, ending with a row 4. The last turn will bring the RS so that it is facing you.

Joining row Yo, knit to yo at end of needle 1 and slip the yo onto the next needle (which has 9 sts on it). Knit the yo and the 1st st of this next needle tog. Knit to last st of next needle (which has 9 sts on it), then slip this last st onto the 1st needle which has the heel sts on it. K2tog (the st just slipped onto the needle and the yo of the previous row). Slip the new st just knitted back onto the last needle – sts will be arranged on the 3 needles as 18, 9, 9.

NEXT ROUND Knit 27 sts, which brings you to the centre of the needle with 18 sts on it, and pm. This will be the beg of the round for the foot section.

FOOT Now knit 15 (20, 28) rnds from the marker – work measures approx 5 (6, 7) cm/2 (2¼, 2¾)" from cast-on edge.

NEXT RND Knit last 9 sts on 1st needle, 9 sts on 2nd needle and 9 sts on 3rd needle.

TOE

Work toe on the next 18 sts of the 1st needle as for the heel, removing marker. After making the last turn, join the toe to the top of the sole with a zigzag cast-off, as follows:

Arrange sts so there are 18 sts on each of 2 needles (i.e. slip the 2 lots of 9 sts tog on 1 needle), 1 needle for the foot sts and 1 for the toe sts. Holding the 2 needles tog with the underside of the foot facing you, p1 from the back needle, k1 from the front needle. Pass the 1st st over the 2nd, *p1 from back,

pass 1st st over 2nd, k1 from front, pass 1st st over 2nd; rep from * until 1 st rem on needle, working last st tog with its accompanying yo. Break yarn and draw tail through last st.

FINISHING

Weave in all tails, making sure the cast-on rnd is joined to prevent a gap.

OPTIONAL TASSELS (make 2)

Cut a piece of card the length you want the tassels to be. Wind yarn of contrast colours around the card to the required thickness. Thread a wool needle with a long length of strong cotton or string, pass it through the top loop and tie tight. Cut the bottom loop and carefully remove the yarn from the card.

Rethread the needle with yarn and wrap yarn several times around the top of the tassel, about 5 mm (¼") from the looped end. Make a few secure stitches over and through this wrapped yarn.

Trim tassels evenly and sew to the top centre back of each sock.

# *Pinafore*

Pair this pinafore with a pretty blouse for a special occasion, or try it with a long-sleeved t-shirt and brightly coloured tights for a more casual look. Unlike many fabric dresses, Baby will find this comfortable to wear and easy to move around in.

Yarn

- Filatura di Crosa Zarina (100% merino extra-fine; 50 g/1¾ oz; 165 m/180 yd): 3 × balls in #1469 dark-grey (MC); 1 × ball in #1493 dark-red (CC).

Needles and notions

- 2 × 3 mm (US size 3) circular needles, at least one of which is 80 cm (32") in length, OR the size needed to obtain gauge

- 1 × 2.5 mm (US size C/2) crochet hook

- markers

- 1 × row counter

- 1 × wool needle

- 2 × 20 mm (⅞") buttons

Sizes

- 0–3 months (6–9 months, 9–12 months)

Knitted measurements

- Chest: 48 (52, 54) cm/19 (20, 21½)"

- Length from top of shoulder: 34 (40, 43) cm/ 13½ (15¾, 17)"

Gauge

- 23 sts and 34 rows = 10 cm (4") in st st.

Notes

- The pinafore is worked in the round on one 80 cm (32") circular needle up to the top of the skirt. Then the bodice is worked on 2 circular needles as explained in the pattern instructions.

- When knitting in the round, place marker 1 st before the last st of each round to prevent it falling off the needle.

PINAFORE

Starting at the bottom edge, with CC cast on 216 (232, 240) sts. Without twisting sts, join into a round and knit 1 round in CC, placing marker at end. Break off yarn.

Join in MC and knit 8 (12, 12) rounds.

Speckle rib band

Rnd 1 With MC, knit.

Rnd 2 Knit.

Rnd 3 With CC, and leaving MC yarn dangling at back of work, *k1, sl 1 pwise; rep from * to end of rnd.

Rnd 4 With CC, *yf, p1 (this is the CC knitted st of the previous rnd), yb, sl 1 pwise; rep from * to end of rnd. Don't cut CC yarn.

Rnds 5 & 6 With MC, knit.

Rnd 7 With CC, and leaving MC dangling at back of work, *sl 1 pwise, k1; rep from * to end of rnd.

Rnd 8 With CC, *yb, sl 1 pwise, yf, p1 (this is the knitted st from previous rnd); rep from * to end of rnd.

All sizes Rep these 8 rnds twice more – there will be 6 distinct rows of CC 'knots'. Break off CC yarn, leaving tail for weaving in later.

Cont to knit every rnd in MC without shaping until work measures 14 (16, 17) cm/5½ (6¼, 6¾)" from cast-on edge.

Decrease row for waist shaping

*K2tog; rep from * to end of rnd.

Note: There won't be enough sts to comfortably stretch out on the 80 cm (32") circular needle, so, as you knit this rnd, divide half the completed rnd onto 2 circular needles – 54 (58, 60) sts on each needle. Place a marker before last st on each needle. At the end of the original rnd where there was previously

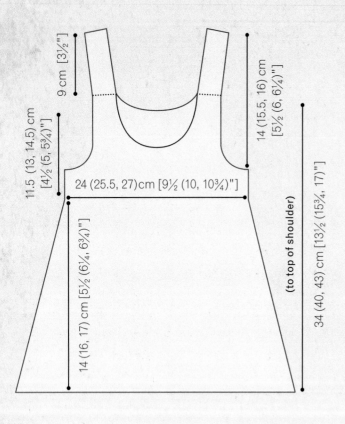

9 cm [3½"]

11.5 (13, 14.5) cm [4½ (5, 5¾)"]

24 (25.5, 27)cm [9½ (10, 10¾)"]

14 (15.5, 16) cm [5½ (6, 6¼)"]

14 (16, 17) cm [5½ (6¼, 6¾)"]

34 (40, 43) cm [13½ (15¾, 17)"] (to top of shoulder)

1 marker, place another marker – a distinctive one so you will know that's the end of a complete rnd. The markers are at each side 'seam'.

Knit the rnds of the bodice by knitting all sts – 108 (116, 120) sts – onto 1 needle, slipping markers as you come to them. Knit the next rnd by knitting all the sts onto the 2nd needle, slipping markers as you come to them.

Cont to knit every rnd without shaping for 4 (5, 6) cm/ 1½ (2, 2¼)".

FRONT ARMHOLE AND NECK SHAPING
Work only on 1st 54 (58, 60) sts, with 1 circular needle. Leave the other 54 (58, 60) sts on the other needle. The front and back are worked back and forth so don't join into a rnd. Work in st st.

Armhole shaping
Cast off 3 sts at beg of next 2 rows.
NEXT ROW Ssk, knit to last 2 sts, k2tog.
NEXT ROW Purl.
Rep last 2 rows 3 (4, 4) times more – 40 (42, 44) sts.

Neck shaping

Row 1 (RS) K16 (16, 17), cast off 8 (10, 10), knit to end of row.

Now cont working on these last 16 (16, 17) sts worked for right front neck shaping.

Right front neck shaping

(see Special Instructions: Make Buttonhole)

Row 2 Purl.

Row 3 (NECK EDGE) Ssk, knit to last 2 sts, k2tog.

Row 4 Purl to last 2 sts, ssp.

Row 5 Ssk, knit to end of row.

Row 6 Purl.

Row 7 Ssk, knit to end of row.

Row 8 Purl.

Row 9 (0–3 months and 6–9 months) Ssk, k2, make buttonhole (over 3 sts), k4 – 10 sts rem.

(9–12 months) Ssk, knit to end of row – 11 sts rem.

Row 10 (all sizes) Purl.

Cont for sizes as follows:

0–3 months

Row 11 Ssk, knit to end – 9 sts rem.

Work 3 more rows in st st.

Special Instructions

MAKE BUTTONHOLE
(This is a single row reinforced buttonhole.)

STEP 1 Sl 1 pwise with yf.

STEP 2 Yb and leave it there.

STEP 3 *Sl 1 pwise, pass previous st over it; rep from * with next 2 sts.

STEP 4 Sl the last st back onto left needle and turn work.

STEP 5 Yb.

STEP 6 Cable cast-on 3 sts.

STEP 7 Cable cast-on 1 more st but yf before placing it on left hand needle, turn work.

STEP 8 Sl 1 kwise and pass extra cable st over it, knit to end of row.

All sizes

NEXT ROW (RS) K4 (5, 5), w&t.

NEXT ROW Purl.

NEXT ROW Knit to end, hiding wrap as you come to it by knitting wrap tog with st on needle above. Cast off all 9 (10, 10) sts.

Left front neck shaping

Rejoin yarn at neck edge with WS facing you and work left shoulder as for right with shapings reversed.

BACK ARMHOLE AND NECK SHAPING

Rejoin yarn at sts set aside for back with RS facing you.

Cast off 3 sts at beg of next 2 rows.

NEXT ROW Ssk, knit to last 2 sts, k2tog.

NEXT ROW Purl.

Rep last 2 rows 3 (4, 4) times more – 40 (42, 44) sts.

Cont in st st without shaping until bodice from waist measures approx 11.5 (13, 14,5) cm/4½ (5, 5¾)".

Begin back neck shaping

Row 1 K13 (13, 14), cast off 14 (16, 16) sts, knit to end of row.

6–9 months

Row 11 Knit – 10 sts rem.

Work 3 more rows in st st.

9–12 months

Row 11 Ssk, k2, make buttonhole (over 3 sts), k4 – 10 sts.

Work 5 more rows in st st.

Work on these last 13 (13, 14) sts worked for left
back neck shaping.

Row 2 Purl.

Row 3 Ssk, knit to end of row.

Row 4 Purl.

Rep these last 2 rows 3 (2, 3) times more – 9 (10, 10)
sts rem. Place a removable marker at end of row to
indicate strap.

On these 9 (10, 10) sts, work about 9 cm (3½")
(approx 30 rows) from marker for strap. Cast off and
remove marker.

Right back neck shaping

Rejoin yarn at neck edge (WS facing you) and
working from row 2, work as for left shoulder,
reversing shaping.

FINISHING

Weave in all tails. With CC and crochet hook, and
beg at a top end of a strap, work a single row of dc
right round neck, armholes and straps. Fasten off
with a sl st and weave in tail. Sew buttons on straps
approximately 2–3 cm (¾ –1¼") from end.

Striped Beanie

This beanie is so easy to make and doesn't take long. It's knitted flat (rather than in the round, like many beanies) and seamed at the end.

Yarn

- Eki Riva Supreme 4 ply (100% SuperBaby Alpaca; 50 g/1¾ oz; 200 m/218 yd): 1 × ball in #1581 diesel (A).

- Shepherd Baby Wool 4 ply (100% pure wool; 50 g/1¾ oz; 165 m/180 yd): 1 × ball in #0097 orange (B); 1 × ball in #0100 blue (C).

- Grignasco Bambi (100% merino extra-fine; 50 g/1¾ oz; 225 m/246 yd): 1 × ball in #185 light-green (D); 1 × ball in #195 red (E).

- Heirloom 5 ply (100% Pure New Wool; 50 g/ 1¾ oz; 135 m/147 yd): 1 × ball in #714 yellow (F).

Needles and notions

- 1 × pair 2.5 mm (US size 2) needles OR the size needed to obtain gauge

- markers

- 1 × row counter

- 1 × wool needle

Sizes

- 0–3 months (6–9 months, 9–12 months)

Knitted measurements

- Head circumference: 41 (44, 46) cm/16 (17¼, 18)"

- Bottom of brim to top of crown (brim upturned): 15 (16, 17) cm/6 (6¼, 6¾)"

Gauge

- 26 sts and 36 rows = 10 cm (4") in st st in Eki Riva.

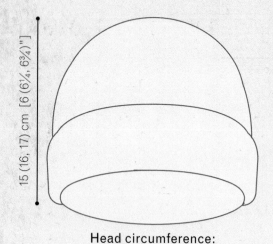

15 (16, 17) cm [6 (6¼, 6¾)]"

Head circumference:
41 (44, 46) cm [16 (17¼, 18)"]

BRIM

Beg at lower brim

Using A, cast on 95 (105, 110) sts.

Row I *K2, p3; rep from * to end of row.

Row 2 *K3, p2; rep from * to end of row.

Rep these 2 rows until work measures about 7 (7.5, 8) cm/2¾ (3, 3¼)" from cast-on edge.

CROWN

Beg striped pattern

0–3 months Using A, work in st st for 2 rows, increasing 3 sts evenly across 1st row – 98 sts.

6–9 months Using A, work in st st for 4 rows – 105 sts.

9–12 months Using A, work in st st for 8 rows, increasing 2 sts evenly across 1st row – 112 sts.

All sizes Cont stripe pattern in the foll sequence, noting knit and purl rows are not always on the usual RS or WS.

With C, knit 2 rows, purl 1 row.

With F, knit 1 row.

With A, knit 1 row, purl 1 row, knit 1 row.

With D, knit 1 row.

With E, *purl 1 row, knit 1 row, repeat from * twice more, purl 1 row.

With A, purl 1 row, knit 1 row, purl 1 row.

With B, purl 1 row, knit 1 row.

With A, knit 1 row.

With C, knit 1 row.

Work should now measure approx 6 (7, 8) cm/2½ (2¾, 3¼)" from where stripe pattern starts.

Beg crown shaping

1st dec row (RS) Cont in C, *p2tog, p5; rep from * to end of row – 84 (90, 96) sts.

Still with C, *knit 1 row, purl 1 row, rep from * once more, knit 1 row.

2ND DEC ROW (RS) With A, *k2tog, k4; rep from
* to end of row – 70 (75, 80) sts.
Next, still using A, purl 1 row, knit 1 row, purl 1 row.
With F, purl 1 row, knit 1 row, purl 1 row.
With A, purl 1 row.
3RD DEC ROW (RS) With D, *p2tog, p3; rep from
* to end of row – 56 (60, 64) sts.
Cont with D, knit 1 row, purl 1 row.
With A, purl 1 row, knit 1 row, purl 1 row.
4TH DEC ROW (RS) Still with A, *k2tog, k2; rep from *
to end of row – 42 (45, 48) sts.
With E, knit 1 row, purl 1 row.
With A, purl 1 row.
With F, purl 1 row.
With C, knit 1 row.
5TH DEC ROW (RS) Still with C, *p2tog, p1; rep from *
to end of row – 28 (30, 32) sts.
NEXT ROW *k2tog; rep from * to end of row –
14 (15, 16) sts rem.
NEXT ROW (0–3 months and 9–12 months) *K2tog;
rep from * to end of row. **(6–9 months)** K1, *k2tog;
rep from * to end of row.
There are 7 (8, 8) sts remaining on needle.
Cut yarn, leaving a long tail. Thread it through all
rem sts and sew tight.

Weave in all threads at ends of rows. With WS
facing you, use mattress st to sew up half the brim
from the cast-on edge of work (this will be the
turn-up), then turn the beanie to RS facing, and
continue to sew to the top of the crown, making
sure all the stripes match. Block lightly over a folded
towel or dressmaker's ham. Do not flatten stripes or
stretch out work too much. Fold up brim.

Bobble Jumper

The shawl collar makes this jumper stylish as well as easy to get on and off. Choose your own combination of yarn colours for the bobbles and stripes, or, for a more subtle textured finish, work in one colour throughout.

Yarn

- Grignasco Bambi (100% merino extra-fine; 50 g/1¾ oz; 225 m/246 yd): 3 × balls in #191 blue (MC); 1 × ball in #184 olive (A); 1 × ball in #185 light-green (B); 1 × ball in #239 aqua (C).

Needles and notions

- 1 × pair 3 mm (US size 3) needles OR the size needed to obtain gauge

- 2 × 3 mm (US size 3) circular needles for collar OR the size needed to obtain gauge

- markers

- 1 × wool needle

Sizes

- 0–3 months (6–9 months, 9–12 months)

Knitted measurements

- Chest: 50 (52, 54) cm/19½ (20½, 21½)"

- Length from top of shoulder: 26.5 (28.5, 31) cm/ 10½ (11¼, 12¼)"

- Sleeve length from underarm: 17.5 (20, 22) cm/ 7 (8, 8¾)"

Gauge

- 26 sts and 38 rows = 10 cm (4") in st st.

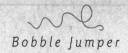

BACK

(see Special Instructions: Make Bobble)

With MC, cast on 67 (69, 71) sts and beg on a WS, knit 3 rows.

Now work bobble bands:

Row 1 Knit.

Row 2 Purl.

Row 3 Knit.

Row 4 Purl.

Row 5 K3 (4, 2), *with A mb, with MC k5; rep from * until 4 (5, 3) sts rem, with A mb, with MC k3 (4, 2). Cut A, leaving a short tail to weave in later.

Row 6 Purl.

Row 7 Knit.

Row 8 Purl.

Row 9 Knit.

Row 10 Knit.

Rep these last 10 rows twice more: on the 1st rep make the bobbles in B and on the second rep make the bobbles in C. Work measures approx 8 cm (3") from cast-on edge.

Now cont in st st until back measures 16 (17, 19) cm/ 6¼ (6¾, 7½)" from cast-on edge.

Special Instructions

MAKE BOBBLE (mb)

[K1, yf, k1, yf, k1] all in the front loop of next st, turn and k5, turn and p5, turn and k1, sl 1, k2tog, psso, k1, turn and p3 tog.

When working the bobble row, weave the bobble colour at the back of work every 1 or 2 sts. By making this short float, the bobble won't be too loose when you purl the next row.

Begin armhole shaping

Cast off 7 (7, 5) sts at beg of next 2 rows – 53 (55, 61) sts rem.

Cont in st st without shaping until armhole measures 10 (11, 12) cm/4 (4¼, 4¾)".

NEXT ROW Cast off 16 (16, 17) sts for shoulder, knit next 21 (23, 27) sts then slip them onto holder for back neck and cast off the last 16 (16, 17) sts for other shoulder.

FRONT

Work the same as for back until you reach armhole shaping.

Armhole and neck shaping

Cast off 7 (7, 5) sts at beg of next 2 rows – 53 (55, 61) sts rem.

Work 4 (8, 6) rows in st st.

NEXT ROW K20 (21, 23), cast off next 13 (13, 15) sts, knit to end of row. There are now 20 (21, 23) sts on either side of the cast-off sts.

Working on the last 20 (21, 23) sts worked for right front, st st 5 rows.

Note: On the right front, neck decreases should slope to the left: on RS of work, dec using ssk.
On the left front, neck decreases should slope to the right: on RS of work, dec using k2tog.

Dec 1 st at neck edge on next row and every foll 6th row 3 (4, 5) times – 4 (5, 6) sts decreased.
Cont to work in st st without shaping on these 16 (16, 17) sts for 5 (1, 1) more rows. Cast off.
Rejoin yarn at neck edge (WS facing you) and work the left front as for right, reversing all the shaping.

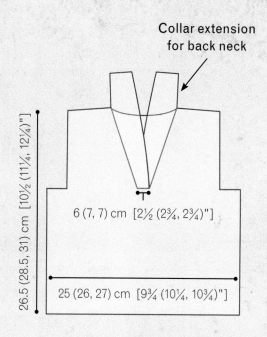

Collar extension for back neck

26.5 (28.5, 31) cm [10½ (11¼, 12¼)"]

6 (7, 7) cm [2½ (2¾, 2¾)"]

25 (26, 27) cm [9¾ (10¼, 10¾)"]

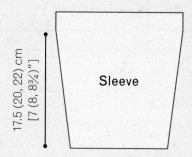

Sleeve

17.5 (20, 22) cm [7 (8, 8¾)"]

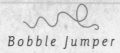
SLEEVES *(make 2 the same)*

With MC, cast on 42 (44, 46) sts and starting on WS, knit 3 rows.

Start cuff stripes now AND AT THE SAME TIME inc 1 st at each end of rows as below.

Note: Increases begin in cuff stripes.

Cuff stripes

Row 1 With A, knit.

Row 2 With A, knit.

Row 3 With MC, knit.

Row 4 With MC, purl.

Row 5 With B, knit.

Row 6 With B, knit.

Row 7 With MC, knit.

Row 8 With MC, purl.

Row 9 With C, knit.

Row 10 With C, knit.

Increases

0–3 months Inc in 7th and then foll 13th row 4 times more – 52 sts.

6–9 months Inc in 5th and then foll 11th row 5 times more – 56 sts.

9–12 months Inc in 9th and then foll 10th row 7 times more – 62 sts.

The rest of the sleeve is worked in MC, in st st and starting with a RS knit row.

Once increases are complete, work 16 (16, 12) rows more in st st. Cast off.

COLLAR

Weave in any yarn tails and block pieces. Sew shoulder seams using mattress st.

Using 1 circular needle and MC, start at right hand front corner, RS facing you, and pick up and knit 21 (22, 26) sts up right front neck, knit 21 (23, 27) sts from back neck holder and 21 (22, 26) sts down left front neck – 63 (67, 79) sts. Don't pick up any of the centre front cast-off sts.

Now, using the 2nd circular needle, work back and forth in k1, p1 rib until collar measures 5.5 (6, 6) cm/ 2¼ (2½, 2½)".

NEXT ROW (1ST SHORT ROW) Rib to last 6 sts, w&t.
NEXT ROW Rib to last 6 sts, w&t.
NEXT ROW (2ND SHORT ROW) Rib to last 12 sts, w&t.
NEXT ROW Rib to last 12 sts, w&t.
NEXT ROW (3RD SHORT ROW) Rib to last 18 sts, w&t.
NEXT ROW Rib to last 18 sts, w&t.
NEXT ROW (4TH SHORT ROW) Rib to last 24 sts, w&t.
NEXT ROW Rib to last 24 sts, w&t.
Now rib 2 rows, hiding wraps as you come to them by working the wrap with the st it wraps.
Cast off in rib using elastic cast-off.

FINISHING

Weave in any yarn tails on collar. Sewing on the wrong side with an overcast stitch, place right sides together and sew down left hand side of collar onto centre cast-off sts at front. Overlap right side of collar on top of left hand collar and stitch down. Fold over collar.

Set in sleeve, sewing the top 2 (2, 1.5) cm/¾ (¾, ½)" section of sleeve into cast-off sts on back and front. Sew up sleeve and side seams, matching stripes and bobbles.

 # Fisherman's Jumper

This fisherman's jumper is warm and cosy – perfect for winter. As it has no neck fastenings, it is most suitable for babies aged 9–12 months.

Yarn

- Eki Riva Supreme 4 ply (100% SuperBaby Alpaca; 50 g/1¾ oz; 200 m/218 yd): 2 × balls in #500 black (MC).

- Grignasco Bambi (100% merino extra-fine; 50 g/1¾ oz; 225 m/246 yd): 1 × ball in #185 light-green (CC).

Needles and notions

- 1 × pair 3 mm (US size 3) needles OR the size needed to obtain gauge

- 1 × set 3 mm (US size 3) dpn

- 1 × cable needle

- stitch holders

- markers

- row counters

- 1 × wool needle

Sizes

- 0–3 months (6–9 months, 9–12 months)

Knitted measurements

- Chest: 53 (54.5, 56) cm/21 (21½, 22)"

- Length from top of shoulder: 26.5 (28.5, 31) cm/ 10½ (11¼, 12¼)"

- Sleeve length from underarm: 17.5 (20, 23) cm/ 7 (8, 9)"

Gauge

- 24 sts and 36 rows = 10 cm (4") in st st in Eki Riva.

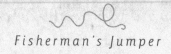
FRONT/BACK (make 2 the same)

With MC, cast on 60 (64, 68) sts using the German cast-on method.

Knit 5 rows, then break off yarn.

NEXT ROW With CC, *K2, p2; rep from * to end of row.

Rep this row 3 times more. Break off CC.

NEXT ROW With MC, inc in 1st st, knit to end of row – 61 (65, 69) sts.

Now beg patt as per charts (*see charts on pages 110–113*).

Note: Place markers between the pattern panels.

WS rows are odd numbered and RS rows are even numbered. Odd rows read from left to right and even rows read from right to left. There are 3 sets of row numbers to keep track of: the entire garment piece, the centre crossed V-cable (14 row rep); and the cables either side of the V-cable (6 row rep).

Row 1 (ws) Work 11 (13, 15) sts in moss st, pm, work row 1 of right cable panel over 12 sts, pm, work row 1 of crossed V-cable panel over 15 sts, pm, work row 1 of left cable panel over 12 sts, pm, work 11 (13, 15) sts in moss st.

Work without shaping in patt as established, slipping markers as you come to them, until 87 (93, 101) rows are completed.

NEXT ROW Cast off 15 (15, 16) sts and break off yarn.

Slip next 31 (35, 37) sts onto st holder for neckband, rejoin yarn and cast off the last 15 (15, 16) sts.

SLEEVES (make 2 the same)

Note: Work all inc sts into moss st panels.

With CC, cast on 41 (43, 45) sts using the German cast-on method.

Knit 1 row. Break off yarn.

With MC, knit 1 row.

(Cont in MC for the rest of the sleeve.)

Begin pattern

Row 1 (ws) Work 9 (10, 11) sts in moss st, pm, work row 1 of cable panel for sleeves over 23 sts, pm, work 9 (10, 11) sts in moss st.

Cont to work in patt as set AND AT THE SAME TIME inc 1 st at each end of 5th and then every foll 7th (10th, 7th) row until there are 55 (57, 63) sts. Cont without shaping until 55 (65, 71) rows have been worked from beg of 1st patt row.

Next row *K2, p2; rep from * to last 3 sts, k2, p1 at the same time inc in this st – 56 (58, 64) sts.

Next row *K2, p2; rep from * to end of row. Cont to work in k2, p2 rib for 4 more rows. Cast off in rib using elastic cast-off.

NECKBAND

Lightly block pieces. Sew shoulders tog using mattress st, matching front and back patterns.

Divide front and back sts from holders onto 3 or 4 dpn, picking up a couple of extra sts where shoulders join. The total number of sts around neck should be divisible by 4 as it will be worked in k2, p2 rib.

With MC, join sts into rnd and work 6 rnds of k2, p2 rib. Cast off in rib using elastic cast-off.

FINISHING

Weave in any yarn tails. Pin the centre st of each sleeve to match the shoulder seam and sew the sleeve, using mattress st, equally onto front and back pieces. Sew side and sleeve seams.

Special Instructions

Note: On charts, all odd rows need read from left to right and all even rows read from right to left.

MOSS STITCH *(see chart)*

(over a multiple of 2 sts plus 1)

Row I (WS) P1, *k1, p1; rep from * to end of row.
Row 2 P1, *k1, p1; rep from * to end of row.

MOSS STITCH

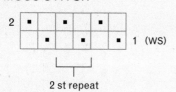

2 st repeat

KEY

k on RS, p on WS	▪ p on RS, k on WS

Right cable: slip next 2 sts onto cable needle and hold at back of work, k4, k2 from cable needle

RIGHT CABLE PANEL *(see chart)*

(over 12 sts)

Row I (WS) P1, k2, p6, k2, p1.
Row 2 K1, p2, k6, p2, k1.
Row 3 P1, k2, p6, k2, p1.
Row 4 K1, p2, sl next 2 sts onto cable needle and hold at back of work, k4, then k2 from cable needle, p2, k1.
Row 5 P1, k2, p6, k2, p1.
Row 6 K1, p2, k6, p2, k1.

RIGHT CABLE PANEL

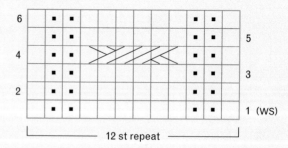

12 st repeat

CROSSED V-CABLE PANEL *(see chart)*

(over 15 sts)

Row 1 (ws) K5, p2, k1, p2, k5.

Row 2 P5, slip next 3 sts onto cable needle and hold at back of work, k2, then sl the purl st from the cable needle back to the left hand needle and purl it, then k2 from cable needle, p5.

Row 3 K5, p2, k1, p2, k5.

Row 4 P4, BC, k1, FC, p4.

Row 5 & ALL SUBSEQUENT WS ROWS Knit all knit sts and purl all purl sts.

Row 6 P3, BC, k1, p1, k1, FC, p3.

Row 8 P2, BC, [k1, p1] twice, k1, FC, p2.

Row 10 P1, BC, [k1, p1] 3 times, k1, FC, p1.

Row 12 BC, [k1, p1] 4 times, k1, FC.

Row 14 K2, p3, k2, p1, k2, p3, k2.

CROSSED V CABLE PANEL

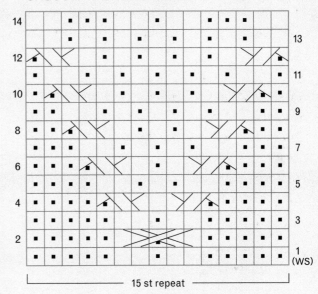

15 st repeat

KEY

	k on RS, p on WS	▪ p on RS, k on WS

 CROSSED V: Slip next 3 sts onto cable needle and hold at back of work, k2, then sl the purl st from cable needle back to left hand needle and purl it, then k2 from cable needle.

 FRONT CROSS (FC): Slip 2 sts onto cable needle and hold at front of work, p1, then k2 from cable needle.

 BACK CROSS (BC): Slip 1 st onto cable needle and hold at back of work, k2, then p1 from cable needle.

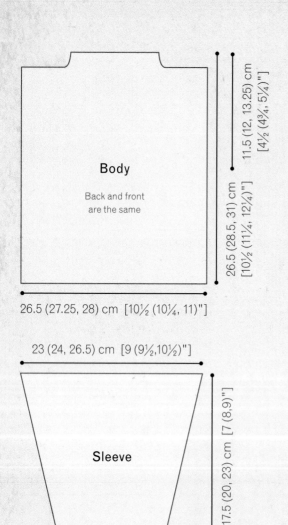

Body

Back and front
are the same

26.5 (27.25, 28) cm [10½ (10¼, 11)"]

11.5 (12, 13.25) cm [4½ (4¾, 5¼)"]

26.5 (28.5, 31) cm [10½ (11¼, 12¼)"]

23 (24, 26.5) cm [9 (9½, 10½)"]

Sleeve

17.5 (20, 23) cm [7 (8,9)"]

LEFT CABLE PANEL (see chart)

(over 12 sts)

Row 1 (ws) P1, k2, p6, k2, p1.

Row 2 K1, p2, k6, p2, k1.

Row 3 P1, k2, p6, k2, p1.

Row 4 K1, p2, sl next 4 sts onto cable needle and hold at front of work, k2, then k4 from cable needle, p2, k1.

Row 5 P1, k2, p6, k2, p1.

Row 6 K1, p2, k6, p2, k1.

LEFT CABLE PANEL

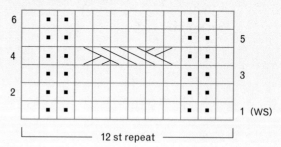

12 st repeat

KEY

| | k on RS, p on WS | | p on RS, k on WS |

Left cable: slip next 4 sts onto cable needle and hold at front of work, k2, k4 from cable needle

CABLE PANEL FOR SLEEVES

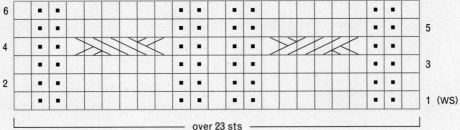

over 23 sts

CABLE PANEL FOR SLEEVES (see chart)

(over 23 sts)

Row 1 (ws) P1, k2, p6, k2, p1, k2, p6, k2, p1.

Row 2 K1, p2, k6, p2, k1, p2, k6, p2, k1.

Row 3 P1, k2, p6, k2, p1, k2, p6, k2, p1.

Row 4 K1, p2, sl next 2 sts onto cable needle and hold at back of work, k4, k2 from cable needle, p2, k1, p2, sl next 4 sts onto cable needle and hold at front of work, k2, k4 from cable needle, p2, k1.

Row 5 P1, k2, p6, k2, p1, k2, p6, k2, p1.

Row 6 K1, p2, k6, p2, k1, p2, k6, p2, k1.

KEY

| □ k on RS, p on WS | ■ p on RS, k on WS |

Right cable: slip next 2 sts onto cable needle and hold at back of work, k4, k2 from cable needle

Left cable: slip next 4 sts onto cable needle and hold at front of work, k2, k4 from cable needle

Terms and Techniques

Note that Australian knitting and crocheting terminology is used throughout this book.

blocking: This process uses steam to give the required shape to your knitting. To block a piece of knitting, first put a thick blanket covered with a sheet on a table (an ironing board can be unstable). Set your iron at the highest wool setting that also allows you to use steam. Place the piece you will be blocking either face down or face up (if blocking multiple pieces, ensure you place them all the same way up) and pin it out to the size the pattern gives for the finished piece. Steam the piece by holding the iron about 2 cm (1") above the knitting, without contacting the piece at all. Shape any edges that are out of kilter. Leave until completely dry before removing pins.

buttonhole: To make a simple buttonhole:
Row 1 Yo, k2tog.
Row 2 Patt 2 sts (working yo from row 1 as a stitch).

cable 4 left (c4L): Sl next 2 sts onto a cable needle and hold at front of work, k2, k2 from cable needle.

cable 4 right (c4R): Sl next 2 sts onto cable needle and hold at back of work, k2, k2 from cable needle.

cable cast-on

1 If there are no existing sts, make a slip knot on the left needle, leaving a long tail. This will be the 1st st.
2 Insert right needle into the slip knot, under the left needle, and wrap yarn as if to knit.
3 Draw yarn through with right needle to create a loop on right needle, then sl this st onto left needle (*see Figure 1*).
Repeat steps 2 and 3 until the required number of sts have been cast on.

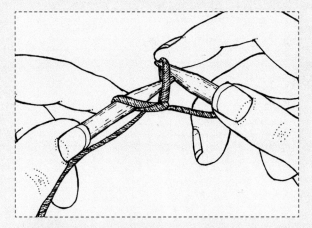

Figure 1

cast on: Unless a particular cast-on technique is specified in the pattern, use any cast-on method you feel comfortable with. The *cable cast-on* and *thumb cast-on* methods are both straightforward.

cast off: Unless a particular cast-off technique is specified in the pattern, use any cast-off method you feel comfortable with. The *cast off knitwise* and *cast off purlwise* methods are both straightforward.

cast off in rib: If the pattern is in rib, this cast-off technique produces a more elastic edge than a knitwise cast-off.

For single rib:

1 Knit the 1st st on the left hand needle and purl the 2nd st.
2 Lift the knit st over the purl st and off the needle.
3 Knit the next st on the left hand needle.
4 Lift the purl st over the knit st and off the needle.
5 Purl the next st on the left hand needle.
6 Lift the knit st over the purl st and off the needle.
Continue in this way until the required number of sts has been cast off.

For double rib (k2, p2):

1 Knit the 1st 2 sts on the left hand needle.
2 Use the tip of the left hand needle to lift the 1st st knitted over the 2nd st knitted and off the needle – 1 st has been cast off.
3 Purl the next st on the left hand needle.
4 Lift the 1st st on the right hand needle over the 2nd st (the stitch just worked) and off the needle.
5 Purl the next st on the left hand needle.
6 Lift the 1st st on the right hand needle over the 2nd st and off the needle.
7 Knit the next st on the left hand needle.
8 Lift the 1st st on the right hand needle over the 2nd st and off the needle.

9 Knit the next st on the left hand needle.

10 Lift the 1st st on the right hand needle over the 2nd st and off the needle.

11 Purl the next st on the left hand needle.

12 Lift the 1st st on the right hand needle over the 2nd st and off the needle.

13 Purl the next st on the left hand needle.

14 Lift the 1st st on the right hand needle over the 2nd st and off the needle.

Continue in this way until the required number of sts has been cast off.

cast off knitwise: All cast-offs in this book are basic knitwise cast-offs unless otherwise specified. To cast off knitwise:

1 With the yarn at the back of work, knit the 1st 2 sts from the left hand needle in the usual way.

2 Use the tip of the left hand needle to lift the 1st st on the right hand needle over the 2nd st and off the needle – 1 st has been cast off.

3 Knit the next st on the left hand needle. Lift the 1st st on the right hand needle over the 2nd st (the st just worked) and off the needle.

Repeat step 3 until the required number of sts has been cast off.

cast off purlwise:

1 With the yarn at front of work, purl the 1st 2 sts from the left hand needle in the usual way.

2 With the tip of the left hand needle, lift the 1st st on the right hand needle over the 2nd st and off the needle – 1 st has been cast off.

3 Purl the next st on the left hand needle. Lift the 1st st on the right hand needle over the 2nd st and off the needle.

Repeat step 3 until the required number of sts has been cast off.

chain (ch) (crochet):

1 Make a slip knot and insert the crochet hook into the loop.

2 Wrap the yarn around the hook from the back to the front.

3 Pull a new loop through the loop on the hook – 1 chain has been made.

Repeat steps 2 and 3 to make required length of chain. (Make sure your left hand is always holding the chain just below the hook.)

decrease (dec): Unless a different decrease is specified (e.g. ssk, ssp), use a simple decrease, as follows: on RS of work k2tog; or on WS of work p2tog.

double crochet (dc): (Equivalent to US single crochet.) Insert the hook into a st, wrap the yarn over the hook and draw the yarn through the work only. Wrap the yarn again and draw the yarn through both loops on the hook – 1 dc is made.

elastic cast-off (suspended cast-off):
This method prevents work from being cast off too tightly, and is particularly good for ***garter stitch***.
1 As with a basic cast-off, knit (or purl) the 1st 2 sts from the left hand needle.
2 With the tip of the left hand needle, lift the 1st st on the right hand needle over the 2nd st – but keep the lifted st on the left needle.
3 Work the next st on left needle (*see Figure 2*) and drop both sts together.

garter stitch: Knit every row.

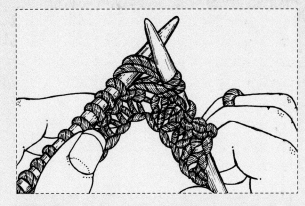

Figure 2

gauge: To check your gauge, knit a test swatch: cast on 30 to 40 stitches using the recommended needle size. Work in the pattern stitch until the swatch measures at least 10 cm (4") from cast-on edge. Remove swatch from needles or cast off loosely and lay on a flat surface. Using a ruler as a guide, count the number of sts across and then the number of rows down (including fractions of sts and rows) that occur over 10 cm (4"). Check over a few different sections of the swatch. If you have more sts and rows than specified in the pattern instructions, use larger needles; if you have less, use smaller needles. Repeat test until gauge is correct.

German cast-on: This cast-on method is particularly good for *garter stitch* as the edge is very even.

1 Start by making a slip knot, leaving a tail of yarn at least 3 times as long as the width you'll be casting on.

2 Holding both strands in your left hand and the needle in your right hand, catch the short strand with your left thumb (moving clockwise).

3 Place the long strand over your left index finger.

4 Insert the needle into the loop around your thumb, from front to back.

5 Catch the long strand going to your index finger with the needle (*see Figure 3*) and draw it through the thumb loop.

6 Drop the yarn from your thumb and pull the short strand, tightening the long strand if necessary. Repeat steps 2 to 6 until the required number of sts has been cast on.

hiding wraps: *see Wrap and Turn*

increase (inc): An increase can be made in various ways, such as through lifting and yarn overs. A simple increase is made by knitting into the front and then back of a stitch.

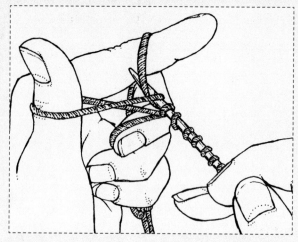

Figure 3

knit (k):

1 Hold the needle with sts on it in your left hand. With yarn at back of work, insert right hand needle into 1st st on left hand needle, from front to back.

2 Take yarn at the back under and over the point of the right hand needle.

3 Draw yarn on right hand needle through st on left hand needle.

4 Slip the left hand st off needle onto right hand needle – 1 knit st is made.

Note: Knitting every row is called garter stitch. The terms 'knitting' or 'knit' can also mean generally

'working' (making stitches) – not necessarily using knit stitch. Thus, to avoid confusion, 'knit' is generally used only when referring to the stitch described above, while 'work' is used in the more general sense.

knit 2 stitches together as 1 stitch (k2tog):

Knit 2 sts tog as 1 st. (This decrease creates a slant to the right when worked on the RS.)

knitting in the round:
This technique involves knitting a tube shape, without any joins, working from left to right continuously without turning the work. It can be performed with 4 double-pointed needles (dpn), or 1 circular needle.

If using a set of 4 dpn, use the following method: using 2 needles, cast on the number of sts specified, then distribute the sts evenly over 3 needles. Form the 3 needles into a triangle, making sure the sts aren't twisted. Have the yarn from the last st cast on at the end of the needle on the right hand side. Join the sts into a round by using the 4th needle and the working yarn from the last st on the 3rd needle to knit the 1st st on the 1st needle. Continue knitting all the sts off the 1st needle, then use the 1st needle to knit all the sts from the 2nd needle. Then knit all the sts off the 3rd needle, using the 2nd needle – this completes the 1st round. A circular needle may be used if there are enough sts to reach from point to point on the needle without stretching the work.

Circular needles come in different lengths and the pattern will specify which length should be used. If knitting in the round with a circular needle: cast on the sts in the usual way, then join them into a round by holding the needle tip with the last sts cast on in your right hand and knitting the 1st st cast on from the left hand tip using the working yarn from the right hand tip. Take care that the sts are not twisted.

knitwise (kwise): *see Slip Stitch Knitwise*

make 1 (m1):
With left needle tip, lift strand between needles from front to back. Knit lifted loop through the back.

make bobble (mb):
[K1, yf, k1, yf, k1] all in the front loop of next st, turn and k5, turn and p5, turn and k1, sl 1, k2tog, psso, k1, turn and p3tog.

markers: Markers are used as visual indicators to mark a certain point in your knitting. They can consist of a loop of contrast yarn, a safety pin, or one of the many commercial markers available – plastic loops, glass beads, silver chains and so on. The marker is placed in the knitting at the point the pattern instructs. When instructed to slip the marker, move it from the left hand needle to the right hand needle.

mattress stitch (ladder stitch): (*see Figure 4*) This stitch is used to neatly join finished pieces together.

1 With RS facing you, use a threaded needle to pick up 1 horizontal strand (loop) between the 1st 2 sts on the 1st piece of work, then pick up 1 loop between the 1st 2 sts on the 2nd piece of work, plus the loop above it.

2 Pick up the next 2 loops on the 1st piece, then the next 2 loops on the 2nd piece.

Repeat step 2 to end of seam. To finish, pick up the last loop (or 2 loops) at the end of the 1st piece and tie off.

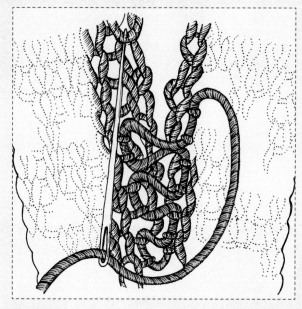

Figure 4

mount: The mount refers to the way a particular stitch sits on the needle. For example, the loop of a knit stitch has its leading edge on the front of the needle.

overcast sewing stitch:

1 Working close to the edge of the fabric, bring the needle through from the back to the front of the work.

2 Take the needle over the raw edges and pass it through the fabric again from the back to the front, 1 st to the left.

3 Continue in this way, making a row of diagonal sts over the raw edge of the fabric. Be careful not to pull the yarn too tight.

pattern (patt): This term is used to describe either instructions for an entire garment (e.g. 'the pattern for the vest') or the stitch design within a garment (e.g. 'the pattern repeat for the vest', meaning the design of the cable). Instructions may say 'continue to work in patt as set', which means you should keep working the garment using the same stitch designs as have been set up in the first instruction rows.

provisional cast-on: A foundation row is cast on in a contrasting yarn, which is later unravelled to free the loops for grafting or picking-up – for example, to form fringes, hems or other edges, or to work in the opposite direction.

purl:

1 Hold the needle with sts on it in your left hand.

With the yarn at the front of the work, insert the right hand needle into the 1st st from right to left.

2 Take the yarn at front of work over and under the point of the left hand needle.

3 Draw the yarn on the right hand needle through the st on the left hand needle. Slip the left hand st off the needle onto the right hand needle – 1 purl st is made.

purl 2 stitches together as 1 stitch (p2tog): Purl 2 sts tog as 1 st. (This decrease creates a slant to the right on the RS when worked on the WS.)

purlwise (pwise): *see Slip Stitch Purlwise*

slip (sl): Unless otherwise specified, sl all sts pwise (*see Slip Stitch Purlwise*).

slip slip knit (ssk):

1 Sl 1 st kwise onto right needle, then sl another st kwise onto right needle.

2 Insert tip of left needle into the front loops of the 2 sl sts (*see Figure 5*), and knit them tog through back loops. (This decrease creates a slant to the left.)

Figure 5

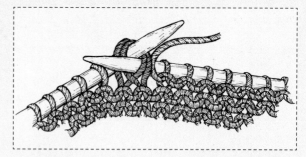

Figure 6

slip slip purl (ssp):

1 Holding the yarn in front, sl 1 st kwise onto right needle, then slip another st kwise onto right needle.

2 Slip these 2 sl sts back onto the left needle.

3 Insert the right hand needle into the back of both sts from left to right (*see Figure 6*), then purl them tog. (This decrease worked on the WS creates a slant to the left on the RS – it is actually an ssk worked from behind.)

slip slip slip purl (sssp):

1 Sl 1 st kwise onto right needle. Repeat twice more.

2 Sl these 3 sl sts back onto left needle.

3 Insert the right hand needle into the back of all 3 sts from left to right, then purl them tog.

slip marker: When instructed to slip a *marker*, move it from the left hand needle to the right hand needle.

slip stitch (sl st) (in crochet): Insert hook into st, yarn over hook and draw loop through st and loop on hook.

slip stitch knitwise (sl 1 kwise): Insert the right hand needle into st on left hand needle as if to knit. Drop the st from left hand needle onto right hand needle.

slip stitch purlwise (sl 1 pwise): Insert the right hand needle into st on left hand needle as if to purl. Drop the st from left hand needle onto right hand needle.

stocking stitch (st st): Knit all stitches on RS of work and purl all stitches on WS of work.

test swatch: *see Gauge*

thumb cast-on:

1 Begin by making a slip knot, leaving a tail of yarn at least 3 times as long as the width you'll be casting on.

2 Taking the needle and long strand in your right hand, and holding the short strand in your left hand, catch a loop of the short strand with your left thumb (moving clockwise).

3 Insert the needle into the loop around your thumb, from front to back.

4 Wrap the long strand under needle (*see Figure 7*).

5 Pass the loop over the tip of the needle, then pull and tighten the short strand, tightening the long strand if necessary.

Repeat steps 2 to 5 until the required number of sts have been cast on.

weave in tails: To hide a yarn tail, use a yarn needle or tapestry needle to weave it either through stitches on the WS of the work (making sure it doesn't show on the RS), or through the loops along the seam edge. Trim tail close to the work, but do not tie a knot, as this may show.

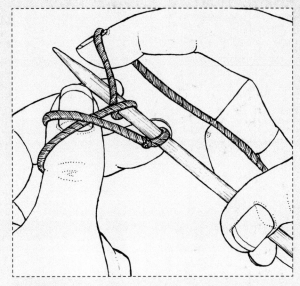

Figure 7

wrap and turn (w&t):

1 At the turning point, sl next st pwise onto the right needle.

2 Bring yarn to front, then sl same st back to left needle.

3 Turn the work and bring yarn into position for next st, at the same time wrapping the st (*see Figure 8*). Hide wraps by working the wrap with the st it wraps. If working in knit stitch, insert right needle under the wrap at the front, and then into the wrapped stitch.

Knit the 2 loops tog. If working in purl stitch, insert the right needle under the wrap at the back, lift onto the left needle and purl the 2 sts tog.

Figure 8

yarn back (yb): Take the yarn from the front to the back of the work between the needles.

yarn forward (yf): Bring the yarn from the back to the front of the work between the needles.

yarn over (yo): There are various ways to make a new st by a yo. Basically, the yarn is wound around the needle to produce a new st. If all sts are knit sts, k1, bring yarn forward and knit the next st taking the yarn over the top of the needle. If the 2nd st to be worked is a purl st, wrap the yarn right around the needle in a full circle.

yarn over backwards (yo backwards): Yarn to back and bring over top of right needle, making a new st.

ABBREVIATIONS

alt	alternate	psso	pass slip stitch over
approx	approximately	pwise	purlwise
beg	begin/beginning	rem	remaining
c4L	cable 4 left	rep	repeat
c4R	cable 4 right	rnd/s	round/s
CC	contrast colour	RS	right side
ch	chain	sl	slip
cont	continue/continuing	sl st	slip stitch (in crochet)
dc	double crochet (US single crochet)	sm	slip marker
dec	decrease/decreased/decreasing	ssk	slip slip knit
dpn	double-pointed needle/s	ssp	slip slip purl
foll	following	sssp	slip slip slip purl
inc	increase/increased/increasing	st/s	stitch/es
k	knit	st st	stocking stitch
k2tog	knit 2 stitches together as if they were 1 stitch	tbl	through back of loop
kwise	knitwise	tog	together
MC	main colour	w&t	wrap and turn
m1	make 1	WS	wrong side
mb	make bobble	yb	yarn back
p	purl	yf	yarn forward
p2tog	purl 2 stitches together as if they were 1 stitch	yo	yarn over
p3tog	purl 3 stitches together as if they were 1 stitch	*	(indicates beginning of a section to be repeated)
patt	pattern/s	–	(numerals that appear after a dash indicate the number of stitches created or on the needle)
pm	place marker	[ ]	(square brackets enclose a section to be repeated)

Suppliers

AUSTRALIA

Black Sheep Wool
118A Bradley Street
Guyra
NSW 2365
website and online shop:
blacksheepwool.com.au

Stock a range of yarns, including Filatura di Crosa, Heirloom, Jo Sharp and Grignasco.

Calico and Ivy
1 Glyde Street
Mosman Park
WA 6012
phone: (08) 9383 3794
email: info@calicoandivy.com
website and online shop:
www.calicoandivy.com

Offer a range of yarns, including Jo Sharp, Rowan and Heirloom.

Craft Den
21 High Street
Mansfield
Vic. 3277
phone: (03) 5775 2044
email: lafolk@bigpond.com
website: www.craftden.com.au

Specialise in quality Australian and New Zealand wool and wool products, and also stock a range of imported knitting yarns, dress-making and quilting fabrics and handcraft supplies.

Greta's Handcraft Centre
321 Pacific Highway
Lindfield
NSW 2070
phone: (02) 9416 2489
fax: (02) 9924 2434
email: vivienne@gretashandcraft.com.au
website and online shop:
www.gretashandcraft.com.au

Greta's Handcraft Centre (continued)

A good variety of yarns is available from the online shop – including Filatura di Crosa, Jo Sharp, Shepherd and Heirloom – with a larger range available from their shopfront in Lindfield.

Knitting Yarns by Mail

website and online shop:

www.knittingyarns.com.au

Offer a good range of Heirloom yarns, as well as a limited selection from Eki Riva and Jo Sharp. They also stock some knitting needles and notions.

Morris & Sons

50 York Street

Sydney

NSW 2000

phone: (02) 9299 8588 or 1800 222 155

fax: (02) 9290 2680

website and online shop:

www.tapestrycraft.com.au

'Australia's largest needlecraft and knitting store' (according to their site), Morris & Sons (previously 'Tapestry Craft') certainly does have a good range of yarns, including: Araucania Ranco, Eki Riva, Filatura di Crosa, Grignasco, Heirloom, Jo Sharp, Rowan, Shepherd and Sublime. In addition, they have an assortment of needles and notions, as well as lots of embroidery and sewing supplies.

Needle Nook

433a Fullarton Road

Highgate

SA 5063

phone: (08) 8271 4670

website: www.needlenook.com.au

Their range includes high quality Australia and New Zealand knitting wools, including merino, mohair and angora yarns. They have comprehensive ranges from Jo Sharp, Heirloom and Shepherd.

Ozeyarn

email: info@ozeyarn.com

website and online shop: www.ozeyarn.com

Stock an extensive collection of yarns from brands including Jo Sharp, Heirloom, Shepherd.

Prestige Yarns

website and online shop:

www.prestigeyarns.com

Importers and distributors of yarns including cashmere, alpaca, angora, wool, mohair, silk and cotton. Brands available include Eki Riva and Araucania. They also stock Knit Picks Options needles.

The Stitchery

1071 Mt Alexander Road

Essendon

Vic. 3040

phone: (03) 9379 9790

fax: (03) 9351 0933

email: info@stitchery.com.au

website: www.stitchery.com.au

This shopfront in Essendon stocks plenty of yarns: pure wool, alpaca, cotton, kid mohair, silks, angora, cashmere, ribbons and metallics. Brands include Jo Sharp, Eki Riva, Filatura di Crosa and Heirloom. They also have an extensive range of embroidery and tapestry threads and supplies.

Sunspun

185 Canterbury Road

Canterbury

Vic. 3126

phone: (03) 9830 1609

fax: (03) 9888 5658

email: shop@sunspun.com.au

website and online shop: www.sunspun.com.au

Yarns available include Rowan, Jo Sharp and Eki Riva. They also stock patchwork fabrics – including Kaffe Fassett's entire range – and a variety of tapestry kits.

Thicket

website and online shop:

www.thicket.com.au

This site only has a few yarn brands, but offers the entire Jo Sharp collection, as well as some organic wools. They also have a range of Fine Clover bamboo knitting and crochet accessories, plus stitch holders and kilt pins.

Threads and More

Shop 7, 637 Sherwood Road

Sherwood, Brisbane

Qld 4075

phone: (07) 3379 6699

fax: (07) 3379 9600

email: shop@threadsandmore.com.au

website and online shop:

www.threadsandmore.com.au

Stock Jo Sharp and Shepherd yarns, as well as a range of other Australian and New Zealand wools. Needles are also available, as well as embroidery threads and ribbons.

Turramurra Drapery

1319 Pacific Highway

Turramurra

NSW 2074

phone: (02) 9449 5843

fax: (02) 9487 8528

email: info@turramurradrapery.com.au

website: www.turramurradrapery.com.au

This shop has been doing business in Turramurra for nearly a century. They stock quilting fabrics, embroidery supplies, and yarns including Heirloom, Jo Sharp, Eki Riva, Shepherd, Grignasco and Filatura di Crosa.

Winterwood Toys

Shop 5, 1–15 Hopetoun Road

Park Orchards

Vic. 3114

phone: (03) 9879 0426

fax: (03) 9879 0427

website and online shop:

www.winterwoodtoys.com.au

With a focus on natural products, this shop offers organic knitting yarns, fleece, pure wool felts, toys, art and craft supplies, and knitting needles.

Wool Baa

124 Bridport Street

Albert Park

Vic. 3206

phone: (03) 9690 6633

email: sales@woolbaa.com.au

website and online shop: www.woolbaa.com.au

Yarns include Filatura Di Crosa, Grignasco,

Heirloom, Jo Sharp and Rowan. They also stock a range of needles and notions, including stitch holders, pompom makers, kilt pins and wool needles.

The Wool Inn

Shop 14, NK Centre, 450 High Street
Penrith
NSW 2750
phone: (02) 4732 2201
fax: (02) 4721 0416
website: www.the-wool-inn.com.au

This shopfront stocks yarns by Filatura di Crosa and Jo Sharp, among others. They also have tapestry and embroidery threads.

Wool Shack

website and online shop:
www.thewoolshack.com

Stock a variety of specialist knitting wool, including organic varieties, and Jo Sharp yarns. They also have a very good range of needles and accessories.

The Yarn Barn

Zanatta Court, 163C St Bernards Road
Rostrevor
SA 5073
phone: (08) 8365 9654
email: info@theyarnbarn.com.au
website: www.theyarnbarn.com.au

Yarns on offer include Jo Sharp, Heirloom, Filatura di Crosa and Shepherd. They also stock a good range of knitting needles, including bamboo, metal, casein and plastic varieties.

Yarnomat

18 Macquarie Street
Williamstown
Vic. 3016
phone: (03) 9397 5059
email: lisa@yarnomat.com.au
website and online shop: www.yarnomat.com.au

Specialising in sock yarns, brands available include Araucania.

Yarns Galore

Shop 3, 17–23 Collie Street

Fremantle

WA 6160

phone: (08) 9315 3070

fax: (08) 9315 3070

website and online shop:

www.yarnsgalore.com.au

This online shop offers yarns by Heirloom, Jo Sharp, Shepherd and Sublime. They're also distributors of German-made Addi Turbo knitting needles and crochet hooks.

Yarns on Collie

phone: (08) 9381 4286

website and online shop:

www.woolshop.com.au

This shopfront offers brands such as Heirloom, Shepherd and Jo Sharp, as well as other Australian and New Zealand knitting wools. They also stock knitting needles, knitting accessories (e.g. stitch counters, stitch holders, pompom makers), as well as tapestry and embroidery yarns and supplies.

INTERNATIONAL

(online stores delivering to Australia)

Abundance of Colour and Inspiration

website and shop:

www.colourandinspiration.com.au

Stock a range of yarns including Eki Riva.

Kaleidoscope Yarns (US)

website and online shop: www.kyarns.com

Stock yarns include Jo Sharp, Filatura di Crosa, and Rowan. They also have an extensive collection of knitting needles.

The Knitting Garden (US)

website and online shop:

www.theknittinggarden.com

This online store offers yarns by Rowan, Jo Sharp and Sublime. They stock Crystal Palace knitting needles (high quality bamboo needles), as well as Addi Turbo needles, crochet hooks and accessories.

Knit World Studio (NZ)

website and online shop:

www.knitworldstudio.co.nz

Brands available from this store include Jo Sharp, Sublime and Rowan. They stock a small range of Addi and Art Viva needles.

Patternworks (US)

website and online shop:

www.patternworks.com

Offer a large range of yarns – including Filatura di Crosa, Rowan and Shepherd – an enormous selection of needles and hooks, and plenty of other knitting accessories.

Royal Yarns (US)

website and online shop: www.royalyarns.com

Brands available include Filatura di Crosa, Jo Sharp and Rowan. Many types and brands of needles are on offer, including bamboo, wooden and steel varieties.

Wool Needle Work (US)

website and online shop:

www.woolneedlework.com

Knitting wools on offer include Filatura di Crosa and Rowan, while a large assortment of needles and notions is also available. They also stock embroidery supplies.

Yarn Market (US)

website and online shop: www.yarnmarket.com

This site has a large number of yarn brands to choose from, including Filatura di Crosa, Rowan and Sublime. There is also a good selection of needles and crochet hooks, as well as accessories.

The Yarn Studio (NZ)

website and online shop:

www.theyarnstudio.co.nz

Specialise in a small number of quality brands, including Eki Riva. They also stock Knit Picks and Art Viva needles.

Felicity Dawson

Felicity Dawson has been designing and making original knitted and sewn garments for as long as she can remember. Her work is particularly influenced by contemporary Japanese pattern-making. A versatile creative type, she studied Professional Writing at Canberra University and is a published poet. She also founded and ran her own film production company, during which time she created diverse costumes for a range of movies. She now lives in Hobart with her husband, where she continues to sew and knit every day, always working on new and challenging projects.

PENGUIN BOOKS

Published by the Penguin Group
Penguin Group (Australia)
250 Camberwell Road, Camberwell, Victoria 3124, Australia
(a division of Pearson Australia Group Pty Ltd)
Penguin Group (USA) Inc.
375 Hudson Street, New York, New York 10014, USA
Penguin Group (Canada)
90 Eglinton Avenue East, Suite 700, Toronto, Canada ON M4P 2Y3
(a division of Pearson Penguin Canada Inc.)
Penguin Books Ltd
80 Strand, London WC2R 0RL England
Penguin Ireland
25 St Stephen's Green, Dublin 2, Ireland
(a division of Penguin Books Ltd)
Penguin Books India Pvt Ltd
11 Community Centre, Panchsheel Park, New Delhi – 110 017, India
Penguin Group (NZ)
67 Apollo Drive, Rosedale, North Shore 0632, New Zealand
(a division of Pearson New Zealand Ltd)
Penguin Books (South Africa) (Pty) Ltd
24 Sturdee Avenue, Rosebank, Johannesburg 2196, South Africa

Penguin Books Ltd, Registered Offices: 80 Strand, London, WC2R 0RL, England

First published by Penguin Group (Australia), 2009

10 9 8 7 6 5 4 3 2 1

Thank you to Nic, Serena, Jantina, Michelle, Claire, Natasha, Jo, Carmen and Isobel, for allowing your bundles of joy –
Charlotte, Tayla, Jethro, Xavier, Joseph, Arthur, Leah, Eliza, Ashley and Louis – to be part of this book.
Thanks also to Prestige Yarns (www.prestigeyarns.com) for their advice and guidance on sourcing appropriate yarns.
We are grateful to Liecel Tverli Scully for granting us permission to base the Felted Booties on her Norwegian House
Slippers pattern, which first appeared in Volume 5 of *Craft* magazine.

Cover and text design by Marley Flory © Penguin Group (Australia)
Illustrations by Marley Flory © Penguin Group (Australia)
Photography by Paul Nelson
Typeset in Grotesque NT Light by Post Pre-Press Group, Brisbane, Queensland
Printed and bound in China by 1010 Printing International Limited

National Library of Australia
Cataloguing-in-Publication data:

Dawson, Felicity
Wrapped in love
ISBN: 9780143006312 (pbk.)
Knitting - Patterns.
Infants' clothing.

746.432041

penguin.com.au